Economic and Social Commission for Asia and the Pacific

Sexually Abused and Sexually Exploited Children and Youth in the Greater Mekong Subregion: A qualitative assessment of their health needs and available services

UNITED NATIONS

New York, 2000

ST/ESCAP/2045

UNITED NATIONS PUBLICATION
Sales No. E.00.II.F.46
Copyright © United Nations 2000
ISBN: 92-1-119995-6

Foreword

Sexual abuse and sexual exploitation of children and youth are issues that urgently need to be addressed in the Greater Mekong Subregion. In addition to thriving cross-border trafficking networks, which lure or force children into prostitution, young people are increasingly entering commercial sex work "willingly", unaware of the conditions in which they work or what the mental and physical consequences will be to them. In addition, socio-economic factors such as lack of education, family breakdown, lack of economic opportunities, and poverty, make young people susceptible to sexual exploitation. Children and youth in the region are also at risk of sexual abuse, usually by someone whom they know and trust. Young victims of sexual abuse and sexual exploitation are at high risk of contracting sexually transmitted diseases, including HIV/AIDS, as well as developing mental and behavioural problems. These children and youth need urgent and skilled social, psychological and medical services. Hence, in addition to critical prevention programmes, specialized services are crucial in order to facilitate recovery.

The prevention of sexual abuse and sexual exploitation of children and youth is a high priority for the United Nations. The Universal Declaration of Human Rights, as well as the International Covenant on Economic, Social and Cultural Rights, call for the protection of children's human rights. Furthermore, international instruments, such as the Convention on the Rights of the Child and International Labour Organization (ILO) Convention 182 concerning the Prohibition and Immediate Action for the Elimination of the Worst Forms of Child Labour, call on States to protect children from sexual exploitation.

In addition to the above-mentioned instruments, the World Congress against Commercial Sexual Exploitation of Children, held at Stockholm in 1996, galvanized the attention of the international community to the plight of sexually exploited children and the need for a global partnership to end the commercial sexual exploitation of children.

Against this background, the member governments of ESCAP, on 30 April 1997, adopted resolution 53/4 on the elimination of sexual abuse and sexual exploitation of children and youth in Asia and the

Pacific. The resolution reflected the firm resolve of the governments of the Asian and Pacific region to tackle the many challenges of preventing and combating sexual abuse and sexual exploitation among its young citizens

The current ESCAP programme is in direct response to resolution 53/4 and the needs of children and youth in the region, with a focus on strengthening the human resources development capabilities of social service and health personnel to assist young victims and potential victims of sexual abuse and sexual exploitation. It is hoped that the present report on the Greater Mekong Subregion will promote awareness among governments, NGOs, and communities at large, of the situation facing today's sexually abused and sexually exploited children and youth. It remains the challenge of all sectors of society to formulate effective responses in order to bring about positive change and the realization of all young people's human rights.

I would like to express gratitude to the Swedish International Development Cooperation Agency (Sida) for financing the ESCAP project on the elimination of sexual abuse and sexual exploitation of children and youth in the Greater Mekong Subregion, as well as for funding the present study. Through its support of this project, Sida has exemplified its leadership and commitment to tackling this issue in Asia.

I would also like to thank the Section for International Maternal and Child Health at Uppsala University in Sweden for the technical support rendered to ESCAP in implementing the project in the Greater Mekong Subregion and in preparing the present study. In addition, the secretariat is grateful to the United Nations Population Fund, the United Nations International Drug Control Programme and the Joint United Nations Programme on HIV/AIDS for their financial and technical support of ESCAP's work in this field in the Greater Mekong Subregion.

Adrianus Mooy
Executive Secretary
Economic and Social Commission
for Asia and the Pacific

Contents

Contents *(continued)*

Message from the Swedish International Development Cooperation Agency

Sexual abuse and sexual exploitation are among the worst violations of the basic human rights of children and youth, and transcend racial, economic, social and regional lines. Although sexual abuse and sexual exploitation are frequently directed towards female children, all children lacking the economic and social status to resist and avoid them are affected. Sexual abuse and sexual exploitation endanger children's mental and physical health and impair all aspects of their development. For this reason, victims of sexual abuse and sexual exploitation are in great need of social and medical services as well as psychological and career counselling. Social and health personnel play a critical role in prevention, as well as the rehabilitation of these victims into society. They are in direct touch with this target group through the provision of services such as health care and are therefore in a position to address the specific needs of the target group.

It is against this background that, in 1998, the Health Division of Sida decided to support the four-year project on combating sexual abuse and sexual exploitation of children and youth in the Greater Mekong Subregion by strengthening national HRD capabilities through training of social service and health personnel. This project is being implemented by ESCAP, in collaboration with the Section for International Maternal and Child Health at Uppsala University in Sweden. The project started with a systematic analysis of the health needs of sexually abused and sexually exploited children and youth and the services that were available to them in all six project countries, after which interventions to combat the phenomena evolved, based on that knowledge.

Sida commends this report, which is among the first comprehensive studies on sexual abuse and sexual exploitation of children and youth in the Greater Mekong Subregion. The report sets out national action in this area, as well as recommendations for action at all levels of prevention. It provides national governments in the participating countries, as well as donors working in the subregion, with a valuable frame of reference for future action.

The priority concern in most countries now is to concentrate the attention of political leaders and policy makers on the urgency of the issue. Only strong leadership can provide the necessary political will to prevent and combat sexual abuse and sexual exploitation of children and youth. I must emphasize the need for substantive implementation of the relevant provisions of the Convention on the Rights of the Child and other related instruments. The Convention, being the most widely ratified human rights instrument in history, offers a unique opportunity to coordinate the efforts of everybody to protect our children and youth.

While we focus on the enormous needs of these children and youth, let us not forget their potential. Children and young people, even when sexually abused and sexually exploited, have the potential to change their world, with conscientious and political support from us adults.

Anna Runeborg
Senior Programme Officer
Health Division, Sida

Preface

The United Nations Economic and Social Commission for Asia and the Pacific initiated a four-year project on strengthening national HRD capabilities through training of social service and health personnel to combat sexual abuse and sexual exploitation of children and youth in the Greater Mekong Subregion in January 1998. The participating countries in the project include Cambodia, Yunnan Province (China), Lao People's Democratic Republic, Myanmar, Thailand and Viet Nam. The Swedish International Development Cooperation Agency is supporting the project activities, and supplementary funding for additional components of the project has been provided by UNFPA, UNDCP and UNAIDS.

The project was formulated in response to Commission resolution 53/4 on the elimination of sexual abuse and sexual exploitation of children and youth in Asia and the Pacific, which was adopted by the Commission at its fifty-third session held in April 1997. The basis for the resolution was a proposal for action by ESCAP member governments at the Asia-Pacific Meeting on Human Resources Development for Youth, held at Beijing in October 1996. The Meeting concluded that there was a lack of information on the situation of sexual abuse and sexual exploitation of children and youth; the health and social services available for those victims and potential victims of sexual abuse and sexual exploitation were inadequate; and social service and health providers lacked training. The current ESCAP project has sought to address all of these identified gaps.

In the first year of the project, ESCAP invited governments of the six participating countries to nominate a government department or ministry to serve as the national coordinating organization for the project. During the same year, each of the organizations carried out a qualitative study to assess the health needs of sexually abused and sexually exploited children and youth and available services. The research findings have been published in six separate reports in English and in the local languages of the participating countries. The resulting national research reports have formed the basis for the development of interventions in the second and third years of the project. The six national reports also constitute the basis for this report, which provides a subregional synthesis of the research findings.

The present report comprises five chapters. Chapter I focuses on the background of the project. Chapter II outlines the current situation of sexually abused and sexually exploited children and youth in the subregion as well as relevant action and legislation. The Greater Mekong Subregion is also introduced in this chapter, which contains an examination of the current socio-economic status of each of the six participating countries. Chapter III presents the study's methodology focusing on the planning and exploratory phases and the problems encountered in each country. Chapter IV presents a subregional synthesis of the causes of sexual abuse and sexual exploitation of children and youth and the health needs of the interviewed children and youth, as well as available health and social services. A country profile of the situation of sexually abused and sexually exploited children and youth, their health needs and the caregivers is also presented by country, as well as an analysis of the gaps in service provision for sexually abused and sexually exploited children, a profile of one victim and a key service organization from each of the six countries. The report ends with Chapter V, which presents the conclusions and recommendations of the study.

This report was prepared by Ms Wanjiku Kaime-Atterhog, expert on children in especially difficult circumstances, who was seconded to ESCAP from the Section for International Maternal and Child Health, Uppsala University, Sweden.

Executive Summary

Sexual abuse and sexual exploitation of children and youth are issues of growing concern in the Greater Mekong Subregion, which includes Cambodia, Yunnan Province (China), Lao People's Democratic Republic, Myanmar, Thailand and Viet Nam. The present report is a synthesis of the needs assessment phase of an ESCAP-sponsored project to combat sexual abuse and sexual exploitation of children and youth in the Greater Mekong Subregion being implemented by government departments in five of the participating countries and by a local NGO in Cambodia. The research, conducted between June 1998 and May 1999, sought to identify common physical, psychological and social health problems of sexually abused children and sexually exploited children in all the six participating countries. Another aim of the study was to explore the services available and identify gaps in services to meet the health needs of the children. In order to carry out these aims, researchers collected and analysed existing information and interviewed doctors, school administrators and other government officials about health services, sexual abuse and sexual exploitation. Researchers also used a semi-structured interview schedule to collect data on 253 sexually abused and sexually exploited girls and boys, in both urban and rural areas.

Overall, children were more likely to be sexually abused by people who were close to them than by strangers. Most of the children had been sexually exploited while working in entertainment establishments, but some had been sexually exploited from their homes, in factories or hotels. In the data collection process, the researchers also interviewed other children at risk, which uncovered evidence of other forms of child exploitation taking place at the research sites.

Ignorance, low educational level, previous history of sexual abuse and premarital sex and lack of social skills on the part of the children made them vulnerable to sexual exploitation. There were also factors at the family level that made children vulnerable to sexual exploitation, such as ignorance, low educational level, poverty, family breakdown and dysfunction and materialism. At the community and societal levels, such factors as the presence and location of traffickers and sex establishments, the demand for virgins owing to fear of HIV/AIDS infection among clients, the high price paid for virgins, environmental disasters, poor working conditions in the factories, lack of awareness and enforcement of laws related to child labour and prostitution, lack of awareness of children's rights, and underdevelopment in rural areas and rapid urban growth, made children extremely vulnerable to sexual exploitation. The research findings from the six countries also showed that children with developmental disability and those with low levels of education were more at risk of sexual abuse. Factors at the family level that contributed to sexual abuse of children were child neglect, poverty, psychiatric illness of a family member, substance abuse by adults in the family, family breakdown and dysfunction. Unsafe school environments and poverty were found to increase children's vulnerability to sexual abuse at the community and societal levels.

The research indicated that the sexually exploited children engaged in behaviour that put them at high risk of contracting STDs, becoming pregnant and suffering from long-term health problems. The behaviour included substance abuse, and lack and misuse of birth control and condoms. Sexually exploited children experienced a wide range of physical and psychosocial health problems, including STDs; HIV; diseases of sexual organs; pregnancy and abortion; injury as a result of physical abuse; feelings of anger; betrayal; sadness; humiliation; shame; rejection; feeling trapped and helpless; suicidal tendencies and self-mutilation; insecurity; indecisiveness; restlessness; quarrelsomeness; low self-esteem; depression; irritability; lying; withdrawal; inappropriate sexual behaviour; destruction of property; aggressiveness and anxiety. Sexually abused children experienced the following physical and psychosocial health problems: occasional colds; peptic ulcers; motion sickness; frequent headaches; stomach-aches; skin problems; malnutrition; fever; dizziness; bedwetting; nail-biting; obesity; hair fallout; epilepsy; seizure from tension; pregnancy; STDs; tearing of genitals; abortion; fear; anxiety; depression; anger; aggressiveness; inappropriate sexual behaviour; hopelessness; daydreaming; post-trauma syndrome; depression; tearfulness; loneliness; self-hurt and attempted suicide.

There are a small number of preventive programmes available to children in all countries, but they exist mostly in the capital cities or urban areas and there are no programmes that specifically address issues or specialized problems related to sexual abuse and sexual exploitation of children in Yunnan Province (China), the Lao People's Democratic Republic and Myanmar. There are few specific programmes in Cambodia, Thailand and Viet Nam, and they are concentrated in urban areas.

Based on the research findings from each country, several recommendations for responding to the health needs of sexually abused and sexually exploited children and youth are provided in this report.

Abbreviations

AIDS	acquired immunodeficiency syndrome
CCPCR	Cambodian Centre for the Protection of Children's Rights
DOLISA	provincial branch of the Ministry of Labour, Invalids and Social Affairs
ESCAP	Economic and Social Commission for Asia and the Pacific
FAO	Food and Agriculture Organization of the United Nations
GDP	gross domestic product
HIV	human immunodeficiency virus
HRD	human resources development
IMCH	Section for International Maternal and Child Health
IQ	intelligence quotient
NGO	non-governmental organization
STD	sexually transmitted disease
UNAIDS	United Nations Joint Programme on HIV/AIDS
UNDCP	United Nations International Drug Control Programme
UNFPA	United Nations Population Fund
UNICEF	United Nations Children's Fund
VD	venereal disease
WHO	World Health Organization

GREATER MEKONG SUBREGION

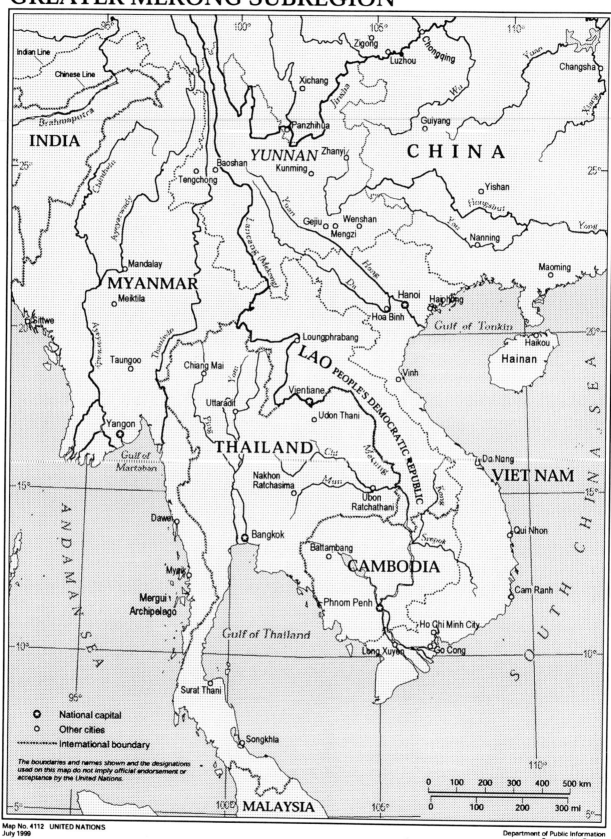

Map No. 4112 UNITED NATIONS
July 1999

Department of Public Information
Cartographic Section

Chapter I

Background and Purpose
of the Project

Although commercial sexual exploitation and sexual abuse of children and youth are illegal in most countries of the Greater Mekong Subregion, they are nevertheless common practices. Commercial sexual exploitation of children in the forms of prostitution, pornography and trafficking within and across borders for sexual purposes occurs largely in the big towns and tourist areas, but also exists in smaller towns and rural areas. Trafficking and prostitution have been serious problems in the subregion for a long time, particularly in Cambodia and Thailand, while pornography is an emerging issue. While all children, especially girls, are at risk, those living in poverty, those that have been abandoned or sexually abused, street children, illegal immigrants, the disabled and those from dysfunctional families are much more vulnerable.

On the other hand, all children are vulnerable to sexual abuse, and there appears to be no regional or ethnic bias in the distribution of this sexual offence against young people. Figures of reported sexual abuse of children and youth in the subregion show that the majority of the victims come from poor families, a finding that has led

---

1 Adapted by W. Kaime-Atterhog from: (a) W. Kaime-Atterhog, "Voices of sexually abused children who live on the streets of Nakuru, Kenya", unpublished report, Section for International Maternal and Child Health, Uppsala University, Sweden (1998); (b) D. Finkelhor, "Current information on the scope and nature of child sexual abuse, *The Future of Children*, vol. 4 (2): 31-53 (1994); and (c) National Centre on Child Abuse and Neglect, *Sexual Abuse of Children – Selected Readings*, Office of Human Development Services, US Department of Health and Human Services, DHHS Publication No. 78-30161 (1980), pp. 1-6.

authorities to associate sexual abuse of children with social disadvantage. However, it is most likely that this is the result of the manner of disclosure, and the extent of sexual abuse among the more advantaged may be effectively concealed. In addition, children of all ages, including infants, are at risk. However, the highest incidence has been noted to occur among children in the 11 to 15-year old group. During those years, children experience rapid physical growth but have limited skills to protect themselves and to seek help. Most of the reported cases of sexual abuse of children and youth occur among girls; however, childcare professionals report that increasing numbers of boys are also sexually abused. In the majority of cases, the main form of abuse was genital intercourse.

The rape of a child by a stranger is the rarest form of sexual abuse. Young people are most at risk from those living with them, related to them or acquainted with them, such as fathers, stepfathers, uncles, older siblings, boyfriends, neighbours and caretakers.

In many countries in the subregion, children are increasingly entering the commercial sex industry "willingly" or by choice on the advice of friends, neighbours and relatives. For most, abject poverty and their financial responsibility as income earners to their families are the primary motives. However, these children do not know the conditions in which they will work, or the consequences of this "choice". The sale of a girl, particularly a virgin, into prostitution brings an enormous sum of money to poor families in the countries of the Greater Mekong Subregion, ranging from US$ 100 to US$ 150. If the girl is very attractive, she can be sold for much higher sums. Once a girl has lost her virginity, her monetary value decreases significantly. In some cases, children are forced against their will to enter the commercial sex sector and are kidnapped, drugged and sexually abused. In Cambodia, the Ligue Cambodgienne pour la Promotion et la Défense des Droits survey conducted in Battambang Province revealed that 65 per cent of the children engaged in prostitution released by the police in the 1995 brothel raid had been trafficked against their will (Seaman 1995).

Trafficking in all countries of the subregion takes place through movement both inside and outside the respective countries. Cambodia and Thailand are both receiving countries and sending countries in the sexual trafficking of children. The most prominent group of non-Khmer child sex workers in Cambodia is the Vietnamese. In Viet Nam, traders will often go to the countryside, where poverty is acute, and lure children into prostitution with promises of a bright prospect of earning a living in Cambodia or China. Most of them are from the south, and enter Cambodia through Svay Rieng. From the border they generally travel to Phnom Penh and are then brought to their final destination provinces. Young Khmer women also leave Cambodia to enter commercial sex work in Thailand via border crossings in Poipet and Koh Kong. Furthermore, girls from Yunnan Province (China), the Lao People's Democratic Republic and Myanmar are lured or trafficked to Thailand, and sometimes on to further destinations.

According to authorities in the subregion, sexually exploited children can be found in brothels, hotels, bungalows, guest houses, tea houses, beer bars, gay bars, go-go bars, folk-dance bars, discotheques, night clubs, pubs, karaoke lounges, cocktail lounges, massage parlours, traditional massage parlours, saunas, coffee shops, cafés, restaurants, beauty salons, male hair salons and as call girls ("free-lance"). The demand for the sexual services of children and youth in prostitution stems from both local men and foreigners, including tourists. Local men in the subregion frequent sex establishments in all provinces in the respective countries, while tourists are concentrated in big urban areas. In Thailand, the demand for boy prostitutes is particularly high among gay tourists. Most boys choose to sell sex to a Western man, as the earnings are higher.

A. MAGNITUDE OF SEXUAL ABUSE AND SEXUAL EXPLOITATION OF CHILDREN

There are no accurate data on the number of cases of sexually exploited and abused children and youth per year and the proportion of young people already affected in specific countries, but indications are that these are growing problems in all six countries.

Little research has been conducted to date on the sexual abuse of children and youth in the Greater Mekong Subregion. It is a sensitive issue and one that is not easily solved owing to a traditional reluctance to intervene directly with other people's family life. In many cases, young victims and their families, out of shame or fear of banishment, do not disclose the crime. In cases where sexual abuse is exposed, it is often not recorded as an agreement is made between the victim's parents and the offender, often with the involvement of officials. Many authorities on the subject report that the pressure on victims of sexual abuse to remain silent or to retract their stories is heavy, and threats of violence are not uncommon. Organizations that offer services to these children may have records of new cases that are reported to them. However, the data are largely documented in an unsystematic manner and reflect specific groups of victims. The police, for example, often only retain statistics on victims who could not settle their case with the abuser. The figures recorded by hospitals reflect the numbers of victims who suffer from severe physical or emotional problems and require treatment. Lastly, social welfare officers may only have statistics of young victims who need social welfare assistance. Thus, the actual number of sexual abuse cases is well in excess of the documented total.

Although the data available on sexual abuse and sexual exploitation of children and youth from service organizations are not comprehensive, they do show that a serious problem exists and that it is growing in magnitude.

The actual number of sexually exploited young people is also difficult to determine with accuracy because many of the sex establishments engaging children are concealed. Children working in the commercial sex sector in many of the countries of the subregion are known to lie about their true age and often have fake identity cards. Some estimates on the number of sexually exploited children in Cambodia and Thailand have been provided by organizations working with these children and are a major factor causing divisions between government authorities and NGOs in these countries. In Cambodia, a survey conducted by Human Rights Vigilance among 6,110 sex workers in Phnom Penh and 11 provinces showed that 31 per cent of the interviewed sex workers were children aged 12 to 17 years. The greatest number of sexually exploited children were found in Phnom Penh and Battambang provinces, where they made up a third of the total. Proportionally, Takeo and Kompong Chhnang surpassed the other provinces, where sexually abused children made up 47.4 and 36.6 per cent of the totals respectively.

In Thailand, NGO figures of children involved in prostitution are as high as 800,000 while government figures put the number at 15,000. Government statistics on children in prostitution are percentages of the adult commercial sex workers. Figures on the latter are based primarily on information from venereal disease (VD) clinics or open commercial sex establishments, and thus those commercial sex workers who do not visit these clinics and those hidden away in closed commercial sex establishments, including many children in prostitution, are not included. Some health officers who treat sexually exploited children do not report the true figures from their surveys on child prostitutes as this may result in conflict with the police owing to the government policy to eradicate child prostitution. The provinces with the highest numbers of commercial sex workers are Bangkok Metropolis and the central region, followed by Chonburi (Pattaya), Songkhla (Hat Yai District), Phuket and Chiang Mai.

4

B. CAUSES OF SEXUAL EXPLOITATION OF CHILDREN

No studies have been carried out on the factors that make children vulnerable to sexual abuse in the subregion. However, some studies exist, mainly in Cambodia, Thailand and Viet Nam, on the factors that influence the entry of children into commercial sex. In Cambodia, the social and economic crisis has created a large supply of young, undereducated and unaware girls, who seek employment to assist their families financially. Owing to the high demand for sex services in the country, young girls are forced or volunteer to sell their virginity for a high price and then continue to work as prostitutes. Boys who live on the street in urban centres have also been sexually exploited by paedophiles in recent years, but they are in far less demand than girls. With the rapid spread of HIV/AIDS throughout the region in the past decade, young girls have been in high demand in sex establishments as many believe that virgins are virus-free and, in the case of old men, that virgins can restore a man's virility.

In Thailand, poverty, community acceptance of the profession, low educational level and lack of skills among children, severe family problems, history of sexual abuse, materialism, and acquaintance with a commercial sex worker are contributing factors. The economic benefit accruing from prostitution has always enticed young people in Thailand. The Thailand study found that each time a prostitute goes out with her customer, she earns at least 500 baht for her sexual services. If she stays overnight with him, she makes B1,500, and the guide who brought the customer to her receives B200 to B300 commission. Salaries in other fields that require minimal education offer far lower wages. The highest minimum wage level in Thailand is currently B162 per day. Many commercial sex workers hope to save money from their work in order to return home to start a family and invest in a small business such as a grocery store or a beauty salon. A recent study on boy prostitutes in Bangkok found that most boys enter prostitution between the ages of 12 and 18 years for monetary reasons, and in some cases, for the sexual experience. These boys live in groups and are often substance abusers of drugs and cigarettes. Sexually, they are known to be promiscuous.

In Viet Nam, cases of girl prostitutes are normally those of girls born in peasant families. Sometimes, a child will see prostitution as an easier way to earn money because it is higher paying than most other available jobs, and will enter the business of prostitution voluntarily.

Because of the new market economy and the rapid economic and social changes in Viet Nam, it has been difficult for the state to stay current and in control of all the latest changes, including the business of trafficking and the prostitution of children and child sexual abuse.

C. HEALTH EFFECTS OF SEXUAL ABUSE AND SEXUAL EXPLOITATION ON CHILDREN

Commercial sexual exploitation and sexual abuse of children and youth result in several physical and psychosocial problems. The limited information available on the health aspects is concentrated on the direct effects of sexual experiences. However, equally important is information on the circumstances leading to the exploitation and abuse and the long-term and intergenerational effects. The direct effects of sexual exploitation and sexual abuse include injury resulting from accidents and physical abuse, pregnancy and STDs, as well as affective, personality and organic mental disorders. Medical doctors working in university hospitals in Thailand, where the majority of sexually abused cases in the country are referred for treatment, report that depression, withdrawal, fear and anxiety are the most common psychological reactions in the victims. Physical signs include vaginal discharge, painful genitalia and pregnancy, while some children have psychiatric problems, including running away from home, post-traumatic stress disorder and withdrawal.

Conditions in the workplace, working hours and the nature of the tasks involved and their consequences are the most obvious characteristics affecting children's physical health and development. The conditions under which children in prostitution live and work in many of the countries of the subregion are reportedly unhealthy and exploitative. In the 1994 survey by the Cambodia Women's Development Association conducted in Cambodia among 399 women and girl prostitutes, 13 per cent of the respondents, when asked about their problems, replied that they "live like animals". Other reports show that these sex workers must be available to serve clients 24 hours a day, whether they are in good or poor health (GAATW 1997). Receiving an average of 5 to 10 customers a day, children in prostitution are extremely vulnerable to STDs. Some common forms found in the countries of the subregion include gonorrhea, syphilis, herpes simplex, urinary tract infections and polyps.

In Cambodia, Human Rights Vigilance reported that the physical health problems of the children in prostitution it surveyed in 1995 included skin irritations, discharges, warts and STDs. The organization sees HIV/AIDS as the biggest health threat to sex workers. Most sexually exploited children have never been educated about, or discussed, sex and do not know their own bodies. In many cases, they have no control over the behaviour of their clients. Moreover, many visit the pharmacy near the brothel for treatment of the disease as, for many of them, mobility is restricted and the cost of visiting a doctor is too high. Some simply have no access to medical care (GAATW, 1997). Girls will only visit a doctor when they are really ill, which in the end increases the expense as their health condition has deteriorated.

D. LEGISLATION AND AVAILABLE SOCIAL AND HEALTH SERVICES

Sexual abuse and sexual exploitation of children are considered crimes under the penal laws of all countries in the subregion and offenders are liable to imprisonment or a fine. Furthermore, all the countries are signatories to the Convention on the Rights of the Child and the majority have national committees on the rights of the child that facilitate the implementation of the laws and provisions of the Convention. With the legislative measures in place, the challenge for countries of the subregion appears to be with law enforcement. In many of the countries, however, these laws are relatively new and methods of law enforcement and judiciary procedures are still being developed. With few exceptions, the police and military in countries of the subregion do not implement laws that protect children from sexual crimes. Instead, in several cases they are actually engaged in the sexual abuse and sexual exploitation of children and youth. According to the UNICEF *The Trafficking and Prostitution of Children in Cambodia: A Situation Report,* there is little doubt that law enforcement officials are involved in practically every stage of the trafficking process (UNICEF 1995). Several locally powerful police and military personnel are known to be involved in both abduction rackets and the protection of establishments which offer the services of child prostitutes. Secondary data from the subregion also point to the fact that many officials and community members, including children, are not aware of these new laws or of the rights of children.

Many organizations are working to end the sexual exploitation and sexual abuse of children and youth in the countries of the subregion as well as to care for the victims of these crimes. The current research project on the health needs and services available to sexually abused and sexually exploited children and youth forms a contribution to these common goals. The few programmes that are in place in the countries of the subregion focus on sexually exploited children. Child rights groups and religious groups have raised fundamental questions regarding the causes, the exploiters and methods of recruitment, the effects on the children and appropriate interventions. They have intervened in communities to prevent more children from being recruited, and they have rescued and cared for those already trapped in the commercial sex industry. This focus has largely been translated into preventive and rehabilitation programmes that are often implemented on a trial and error basis.

E. THE CURRENT ESCAP PROJECT

Few systematic studies have been undertaken in the subregion with a view to understanding the phenomenon and evolving strategies to prevent and combat sexual abuse and sexual exploitation of children and youth based on that knowledge. Moreover, caregivers have not received adequate training to enable them to address the needs of the victims of sexual exploitation and sexual abuse and their families. The current project addresses these gaps.

In the first phase of the project, ESCAP invited the governments of all the six countries to nominate a focal point for the project. For some of the governments, the existence of child sexual abuse and sexual exploitation had not even been openly accepted. Thus, some governments were initially reluctant to nominate any government counterpart, for to do so would be to admit that such problems did exist in their own country. Though it is true that certain organizations, particularly NGOs, had been working in these areas for many years, it was felt that governmental recognition and acceptance from the beginning and throughout all subsequent phases of the project activities would enable policy changes to be made and thus facilitate the greatest impact to the beneficiaries – the victims and/or potential victims of sexual abuse and sexual exploitation. In fact, some of the governments that were contacted were initially reluctant to appoint any government focal point for the project precisely because of the sensitive nature of the project topics.

The next step in the first year of the project was to conduct qualitative research in each of the six countries of the subregion, to determine the situation of sexually abused and sexually exploited children, focusing on their comprehensive health needs and available services. The resulting national research reports form the basis for the development of interventions in the second and third years of the project. In addition, collaborative linkages and networking among government agencies, research institutes and NGOs working to combat sexual abuse and sexual exploitation of children and youth in the subregion were established. In the same year, a film entitled "No is Not Enough" was produced and used to sensitize policy makers about the needs and problems of this group of children with a view to supporting policies and programmes to improve access to relevant health and social services.

The second phase of the project activities, in the second year, were initiated at national HRD workshops on sexual abuse and sexual exploitation among youth, which were held in all six participating countries. The workshops, attended by up to 60 health and social service care providers from concerned government ministries and NGOs, as well as United Nations agencies, were organized jointly by ESCAP and each of the national focal points. The objectives of the workshops were threefold: (1) to share the findings and recommendations of the qualitative research; (2) to identify the training needs of health and social service providers; and (3) to develop a pilot project to follow up on some recommendations of the research. The training needs assessments have been used in the development of curriculum and training materials to enhance the capacity of social service and health professionals to deal with sexually abused and sexually exploited children and youth. In addition, community-level pilot projects are being implemented this year to follow up the recommendations of the research as well as to raise awareness among community members of the health implications of sexual abuse and sexual exploitation for children.

The third and fourth years, comprising the last phase of the project, will focus on the conduct of the subregional ESCAP HRD Course on Medical and Psychosocial Services for Sexually Abused and Sexually Exploited Children and Youth to assess the applicability of the course curriculum developed during the second year. The curriculum and training materials, which will be translated into national languages, will provide input for the training of other social services and health personnel, and allow for project sustainability and improved services to sexually abused and sexually exploited children and youth. As follow-up to the course, country teams will implement pilot projects over a period of eight months, which will aim to improve the access of sexually abused and sexually exploited children and youth to relevant health and social services, as well as educational and training opportunities. In addition, the pilot projects will increase awareness among institutions, both governmental and non-governmental, of the need to prevent sexual abuse and sexual exploitation of children and youth.

The conduct of the ESCAP Course will produce a pool of competent social service and health personnel whose improved performance will lead to better service delivery. This pool of qualified personnel could in turn train other service providers at the community level.

F. RESEARCH REPORT

The following report provides a synthesis of the situation relating to child and youth sexual abuse and sexual exploitation in the six participating countries. It is based on the national reports of Cambodia, Yunnan Province (China), Lao People's Democratic Republic, Myanmar, Thailand and Viet Nam. National research teams composed of government agencies and NGOs and/or academic institutions have carried out the national research and written the reports, with assistance from ESCAP. The research had the following objectives:

(1) To collect and analyse existing information on the country context, sexual abuse (rape and incest) and sexual exploitation (trafficking, pornography and prostitution);

(2) To identify the common health (medical, psychological and social) problems and needs of sexually abused and sexually exploited children; and

(3) To explore the range of services available to sexually abused and sexually exploited children and the capacity and potential of the different agencies in providing such services.

The starting point for the reports has been that commercial sexual exploitation and sexual abuse of children and youth are a violation of the rights of young people, with far-reaching consequences for their health and well-being. The basic premise is enshrined within the Convention on the Rights of the Child which, in articles 19, 34 and 35, requires States Parties to protect children from abuse and neglect, sexual exploitation and sale, trafficking and abduction. Article 33 states that States Parties shall take all appropriate measures, including social and educational measures, to protect children from the illicit use of narcotic drugs and psychotropic substances. This problem is closely linked to the health of children in prostitution and those living and working on the streets.

The Convention also addresses issues related to the provision and quality of health services. In article 24, children have the right "to the enjoyment of the highest attainable standard of health". In addition, article 3 states that the best interests of the child shall be a primary consideration in all actions concerning children, and it emphasizes the responsibility of States Parties to have a good standard of health care: "States Parties shall ensure that the institutions, services and facilities responsible for the care and protection of children shall conform with the standards established by competent authorities, particularly in the areas of safety, health, in the number and suitability of their staff, as well as competent supervision". The text in article 39 is clear regarding the factors that are crucial for effective rehabilitation programmes for sexually exploited and sexually abused children: "States Parties shall take all appropriate measures to promote physical and psychological recovery and social reintegration of a child victim of: any form of neglect, exploitation, or abuse; torture or any other form of cruel, inhuman or degrading treatment or punishment; or armed conflicts. Such recovery and reintegration shall take place in an environment which fosters health, self-respect and dignity of the child".

G. DEFINITIONS

It is necessary from the very onset to define some terms that will be referred to throughout the report. To define a child, the research uses article 1 of the Convention on the Rights of the Child, which defines a child as, "every human being below the age of 18 years, unless, under the law applicable to the child, majority is attained earlier". According to the national laws of the participating countries there are numerous age brackets and definitions of what constitutes a child and his/her rights and responsibilities as a citizen. In many of the countries, children are considered to be those citizens aged less than 16 years old. However, for the purpose of this research project, a person under the age of 18 years is considered a child. This definition of a child overlaps with the United Nations definition of "youth", which covers the age range of 15 to 24 years.

Sexual abuse of children can be defined as contacts or interactions between a child and an older or more knowledgeable child or adult (stranger, sibling, or person in positions of authority, such as parent or caretaker) when the child is being used as an object for the older child or adult's sexual needs. These contacts or interactions are carried out against the child using force, trickery, bribes, threats or pressure. The two forms of sexual abuse that were considered in this study are rape, which is defined as any sexual behaviour imposed on a child by a stranger, and incest, defined as any sexual behaviour imposed on a child by a member of either the immediate or extended family. The extended family includes people whom the child or family has known for a significant length of time and whom they trust, such as fathers, stepfathers, uncles, siblings and other family members, as well as friends, neighbours, teachers, doctors and members of religious communities. Broadening the concept of incest beyond close blood relatives is very important. It helps underscore the special harm caused by any sexual activity between a person in a position of status, trust and authority, and a child in a position of dependency.

Sexual abuse can be physical, verbal or emotional, and includes:

Physical sexual abuse: touching and fondling of the sexual portions of the child's body (genitals and anus) or touching the breasts of pubescent females, or the child's touching the sexual portions of a partner's body; sexual kissing and embraces; penetration, which includes penile, digital and object penetration of the vagina, mouth or anus; masturbating a child or forcing the child to masturbate the perpetrator.

Verbal sexual abuse: sexual language that is inappropriate for the age of the child, used by the perpetrator to generate sexual excitement, including making lewd comments about the child's body and making obscene phone calls.

Emotional sexual abuse: use of a child by a parent or adult to fill inappropriate emotional needs, thereby forcing the child to fulfil the role of a spouse.

Exhibitionism and voyeurism: having a child pose, undress or perform in a sexual fashion on film or in person (exhibitionism); and "peeping" into bathrooms or bedrooms to spy on a child (voyeurism); exposing children to adult sexual activity or pornographic movies and photographs.

Commercial sexual exploitation of children is defined by the United Nations as the use of a child for sexual purposes in exchange for cash or in-kind favours between the customer, intermediary or agent and others who profit from the trade in children for these purposes (parent, family member, procurer, teacher etc).

There are three forms of commercial sexual exploitation of children which have already been defined by the United Nations: child prostitution, trafficking and sale of children across borders and within countries for sexual purposes and pornography.

Child prostitution is the act of engaging or offering the services of a child to a person to perform sexual acts for money or other consideration with that person or any other person.

Trafficking and sale of children across borders and within countries for sexual purposes is the transfer of a child from one party to another for whatever purpose in exchange for financial consideration or other rewards. Sexual trafficking is the profitable business of transporting children for commercial sexual purposes. It can be across borders or within countries, across state lines, from city to city, or from rural to urban centres.

Child pornography is visual or audio material which uses children in a sexual context. It consists of the visual depiction of a child engaged in explicit sexual conduct, real or stimulated, or the lewd exhibition of the genitals intended for the sexual gratification of the user, and involves production, distribution and/or use of such material.

This proposed course model has been successfully implemented in South Asia and Africa by the Section for International Maternal and Child Health of Uppsala University in Sweden, which is cooperating with ESCAP in this project.

Chapter II

The Project Countries

A. AN OVERVIEW OF THE GREATER MEKONG SUBREGION[2]

The Greater Mekong Subregion, covering a land area of approximately 2.3 million square kilometres, has a population of about 237 million people.

The countries of the subregion, Cambodia, China, Lao People's Democratic Republic, Myanmar, Thailand and Viet Nam, all share the Mekong River, which defines the subregion. Natural resources abound, including a rich agricultural base, extensive timber and fisheries resources, considerable mineral potential, and vast energy resources in the form of hydropower and large coal and petroleum reserves. Proper management practices will be critical to ensure the sustainable development of these natural resources.

There is a large labour pool in the subregion, much of which is underemployed and hence available for light industry and other opportunities. The labour force is low-wage, young and industrious. There is a strong willingness to learn, and investment in education and training has high returns. Foreign investors have recognized the great potential of the subregion; joint ventures with domestic enterprise and other investment forms have led to major export gains.

The countries of the subregion are in transition from centrally planned, inward-looking economies to more market-based, open economies. GDP of the subregion is estimated to have been around

---

[2]   This section is derived from material from the Asian Development Bank.

Table. Key population, social and economic indicators of the Greater Mekong Subregion
1996

	Cambodia	Yunnan Province (China)	Lao People's Democratic Republic	Myanmar	Thailand	Viet Nam
Population	11 million	40.8 million	4.8 million	46.4 million	60.6 million	75.7 million
Land area	181 000 sq km	394 000 sq km	237 000 sq km	677 000 sq km	513 000 sq km	332 000 sq km
GDP per capita	$282	$479	$357	$172	$2,543	$330
Real GDP growth rate	2.0%	8.8%	6.5%	5.0%	-0.4%	8.8%
Population % female	52.2	49.2	50.6	50.3	50.1	N/A
Population % aged 0-14	43.9	26.3	44	33.5	27	36
Population % rural	85.6	70.6	83	N/A	81.6	79
Life Expectancy years	50.3/58.6	68.0/71	51/52	60.4/63.4	67/72	66/69
Adult literacy rate-%	81.8/58	89.9/74.5	74/49	89/78	96/92	97/91
Population employed (thousands)	4 939	688 500	2 160	17 964	32 232/5,6	35 800
Percentage employed in agriculture	81.6	50.5	85.5	63.4	50.0/5,6	69.3
Percentage Female labour force	53.2	..	52	..	..	..

Source: The sources for the first four items is Asian Development Bank, "Facts & Figures" of the ADB Online – Greater Mekong subregion web page.

The rest are from ESCAP, *Asia-Pacific in Figures 1998* (ST/ESCAP/1937).

Note: The more recent 1997 figures were available for some facts of some countries, but the 1996 figures were used to maintain uniformity across all figures.

The figures of population, land area, GDP per capita, and real GDP growth rate are specifically for Yunnan Province, as provided by ADB, but the other figures are for China as a whole as provided by *Asia-Pacific in Figures 1998*.

Two dots (..) indicate that data are not available.

US$ 238 billion in 1996. GDP per capita ranges from US$ 280 to US$ 3,100, or an average of about US$ 800. Thailand has the highest per capita income due to its high period of economic growth. Cambodia, the Lao People's Democratic Republic, Myanmar, Viet Nam and Yunnan Province (China) are now also experiencing growth rates of 6 to 10 per cent (1996). If these economies continue to perform well, the total GDP of the region will reach US$ 863 billion by 2010. This means that if the population growth in the region is held at 2 per cent, the subregion will have 314 million people by 2010 and an average per capita income of over US$ 2,700, more than triple the 1996 level.

Combined with rural/urban shifts, the population momentum in the countries and areas of the subregion will add more than 100 million to its major cities and towns. The consumer market will grow exponentially, as poverty declines and people seek to gain the benefits of modernization. Per capita incomes could triple or quadruple over the period to 2020. Major structural changes will also sweep the subregion. Agriculture will decline in importance, as industrial output is expected to continue to grow at two to three times the rate of agricultural output.

Deservedly, and despite the recent economic crisis, the subregion is increasingly recognized as a new area for growth in Asia. Environmental, income distribution, infrastructure, human resources and other concerns pose serious challenges for the subregion, but domestic and foreign resources, including external assistance, are combining effectively to build the basis for more sustained rapid growth.

B. COUNTRY OVERVIEWS

1. Cambodia

Cambodia covers a land area of 181,035 square kilometres and is bounded on the west by Thailand, on the north by Thailand and the Lao People's Democratic Republic, on the east and south-east by Viet Nam, and on the south by the Gulf of Thailand. Cambodia's total population was 10.4 million in 1995, 4,822,000 of whom were under 18 years of age, and it is estimated that it will reach 12 million by 2000. According to official statistics, around 96 per cent of the population living in Cambodia are ethnic Khmers (ethnic Cambodians), making the country the most homogeneous in South-East Asia. The Vietnamese are the largest non-Khmer ethnic group in the country. Other non-Khmer ethnic groups include ethnic Chinese, Cham Muslims and ethno-linguistic minorities. The majority of the people of

Cambodia are Buddhists. The country is facing big challenges in the struggle against the sexual abuse and sexual exploitation of its children. The political turmoil of the past two and a half decades has torn the economic and social fabric of the country apart, creating a breeding ground for illegal activity, including crimes against children.

Cambodia is one of the poorest countries in the world (UNICEF 1998). Its human development index currently ranks 140 out of a total of 172 countries. Other development indicators, such as the maternal mortality rate, infant mortality rate and under-five mortality rate, reflect the same pattern, at 900 per million live births, 108 per thousand live births, and 170 per thousand live births respectively in 1996 (UNICEF 1998). In the period 1990-1995, only 53 per cent of the population had access to health services and 14 per cent to sanitation facilities (UNDP 1998).

Sex-disaggregated development indicators show that men and women have experienced poverty differently in Cambodia. In 1995, the life expectancy at birth for women was 51.9 years, while men lived an average of 56.9 years (UNDP 1998). Education statistics for the same year indicated similar differences by sex. The adult literacy rate was 80 per cent for men but only 53 per cent for women (UNICEF 1998). Similarly, the primary school gross enrolment ratio was 122 per cent and the female rates as a percentage of male, 81. Finally, the secondary school gross enrolment ratio was 27 per cent and the female rate as a percentage of the male rate, 59.

That Cambodian women have had significantly fewer educational opportunities than men is one indication of the varying roles of men and women in society. Boys have traditionally been encouraged to go to school and develop a trade, whereas girls have been raised to help their mothers with domestic chores and childcare. A girl, it was presumed, would eventually marry and raise children, and thus would have no use for an education. Once married, a daughter resides with her parents and is responsible for supporting them. A son does not have the same obligation.

Differentiated gender roles also exist with regard to sexual behaviour. Traditionally, men were polygamous, and wealthy men had several wives. Today, Cambodian men keep the old tradition of multiple sexual partners alive by visiting sex workers. A study conducted by World Vision International in 1994, and another by the Cambodian Red Cross in 1997, showed that the men surveyed had had sex with a prostitute in the last year at rates of 41 and 22 per cent respectively (CRC/ARC 1997).

18

Sex for men before marriage is sanctioned by society. By contrast, social norms dictate that women should be monogamous and that they should remain virgins until they are married. A girl who deviates from this norm, even if she is raped, is shunned by society and is deemed unfit for marriage and suited for prostitution. In many cases, the reputation of the girl's sisters is also tainted, and they find it difficult to find a spouse.

During the Pol Pot years from 1975 to 1979, the ruling and educated classes were targeted in a genocide campaign of enormous magnitude. A third of the Cambodian population perished in those four years. When the Vietnamese took hold of power in 1979, hundreds of thousands of survivors made their new homes in refugee camps along the border with Thailand and in third countries. Those who remained in the country suffered from extreme poverty, lacking support from their families, the State and the international community.

At the height of the cold war in 1979, Cambodia was denied Western assistance because of its leadership, which stayed in power until 1989. Concurrently, civil strife raged on between national factions. A United Nations-brokered agreement in 1991 tempered the civil conflict, paved the way for the 1993 national elections, administered by the United Nations Transitional Authority in Cambodia (UNTAC), and put an end to the international isolation of the country.

2. Yunnan Province (China)

Situated in the south-west of China, Yunnan Province occupies a total area of 394,000 square kilometres, ranking eighth largest in the country. It borders on the two provinces of Quangxi and Guizhou in the east, Sichuan Province in the north, Tibet Autonomous Region in the north-west, Myanmar in the west, the Lao People's Democratic Republic and Viet Nam in the south, and is very close to Thailand and India. Yunnan Province has a boundary line 4,060 km long, of which the Yunnan-Myanmar boundary line is 1,997 km long, the Yunnan-Lao People's Democratic Republic line 710 km long and the Yunnan-Viet Nam line, 1,353 km long.

Yunnan Province is abundant in natural resources and reputed as being the "kingdom of plants" and the "kingdom of animals". In addition, it is a multinational province with many different ethnic populations. The population growth was approximately 1.3 per cent in 1997, with a total population of 40.9 million; 33.23 per cent of the population is composed of ethnic groups. There are 25 different ethnic groups.

In 1997, Yunnan Province had a GDP of 164.426 billion yuan, constituting 2.2 per cent of the total GDP for China, and ranking eighteenth in the country. Yunnan Province is a popular tourist destination; in 1997, the number of international tourists increased by 9.6 per cent over the previous year.

The whole province made an annual investment of five billion yuan in its educational undertakings. By the end of 1997, there was an attendance rate of school-age children of 98.36 per cent, and pupils' rate of admission into higher school of 76.05 per cent. It has also implemented a massive literacy campaign, and lowered its illiteracy rate to 14 per cent.

As Yunnan Province is a frontier and mountainous province inhabited by many ethnic groups, there is a great disparity between one district and another as regards natural condition, social customs and habits, economic and cultural bases and the level of social development, resulting in a big gap between one district and another in the level of culture and education.

In overall cultural quality, the city of Kunming ranks the highest while Simao, Xishuangbanna and Lincang rank among the lowest. Eighty-eight per cent of the highly educated people live in cities and towns, with only 12 per cent in the rural areas. This phenomenon indicates that the structure of culture and education for villages remains at a lower level. In the attendance rate of population, the rate of urban school-age children's admission into primary schools (91 per cent), that of urban students' admission into high schools (61.6 per cent) and that of urban students' admission into universities or colleges (7.8 per cent) are in stark contrast to that of rural school-age children, where the rates are 71, 15.8 and .10 per cent respectively. This poses major challenges for the government in the rural areas.

3. Lao People's Democratic Republic

The Lao People's Democratic Republic is a small landlocked country with a land area of 236,000 sq km. The country is bordered to the east by Viet Nam, to the west by Thailand, to the south by Cambodia, and to the north by China and Myanmar. Known in antiquity as Lan Xang (Million Elephants), the Lao People's Democratic Republic is finally enjoying peace after nearly 300 years of war with Annam, China, France, Thailand, and the United States of America. Following the official takeover in 1975 by the People's Revolutionary Party, the official name of the country was changed to the Lao People's Democratic Republic.

In 1997, the population of the Lao People's Democratic Republic was 4,845,800, coming from 47 ethnic groups. Almost 55 per cent of the population is below 19 years of age and women of reproductive age make up 23 per cent of the total population. More than half of the population (65 per cent) is Buddhist. The majority of the population live along the bank of the Mekong River and 80 per cent of the population are engaged in agriculture, fishing and forestry; another 10 per cent are employed in the armed forces or the civil services. This breakdown remained the same before and after the Revolution.

Modern Lao history began 600 years ago, when Chao Fa Ngum founded the unified country of Lan Xang in 1353 and built it into a prosperous land. The Lao People's Democratic Republic enjoyed relative peace and prosperity for almost 500 years until the mid-eighteenth century, when it was repeatedly threatened and invaded by outside powers.

In the 1900s, under the leadership of the former Indochinese Communist Party and the present Lao People's Revolutionary Party, the multi-ethnic Lao people carried out a long struggle for independence. The Lao People's Democratic Republic was established on 2 December 1975, thus opening a new era in the country.

In the past two decades, the Government has paid close attention to developing its infrastructure for education and public health. Every Lao citizen is required to complete the first five years of primary school and is not required to pay fees for attending public schools. Access to education in the remote mountain areas, however, is limited. Nearly one third of the school-age population (27 per cent) are not enrolled in the education system and the general illiteracy rate for Lao people is 35 per cent. To address these problems, the Ministry of Education has implemented major reforms in order to improve teacher quality and to increase access to education for all ethnic groups.

The Government has also made great efforts to improve the public health system throughout the country. Since 1975, mortality rates have decreased and the Government has established programmes and policies that incrementally address the health-care needs of the people. Services, however, remain insufficient, especially in the remote areas, where the communication and access to health-care facilities is difficult. Lao children continue to suffer and die from common diseases, such as diarrhoea, malaria and respiratory infections. The current life expectancy is 51 years for men and 53 years for women.

The Lao People's Democratic Republic is a country with a strong foundation in culture and tradition. Although the national language is officially Lao, each ethnic minority group maintains its own cultural traditions and languages. In the ethnic Lao tradition, residence and household formation are commonly matrilocal, in that a husband will move to live with his wife's family and land and households are generally inherited by daughters, who are expected to care for their parents. However, men are still often considered the head of the household. This traditional status for women does not apply for other ethnic groups, which make up half the country's population.

Since the official adoption of the New Economic Mechanism in 1986, economic reforms have been pursued with great speed and intensity in the Lao People's Democratic Republic. The essence of the Mechanism has been a shift towards market determination of prices and resource allocation, and the adoption of indicative planning, accompanied by decentralization of control over industries (including privatization) and deregulation to create an open climate for trade and investment through economic liberalization. Economic policies have all been reform-oriented and will continue to be so to enhance sound macroeconomic management and stability, maintain high growth rates and establish the legal, regulatory, administrative and institutional framework needed for a market economy to function efficiently, including the opening up of the economy to regional integration.

4. Myanmar

Myanmar, with its capital city Yangon, has a land area of 676,577 sq km. The country shares international borders with Bangladesh and India to the west, and China, the Lao People's Democratic Republic and Thailand to the east. The Andaman Sea and the Gulf of Martaban are situated to the south of the country and the Bay of Bengal is to its west. Myanmar has a 2,228-km coastline, which includes the Rakhine Coast, the Delta Region and the Tanintharyi Coastal Strip.

The total estimated population of Myanmar was 47,250,000 inhabitants in 1998, and males outnumbered females by 330,000. The population structure consisted of 15,240,000 people under 15 years of age, 26,860,000 between the ages of 15 and 59 years, and 3,460,000 exceeding 60 years of age.

Myanmar is made up of 135 ethnic groups, of which the major ones include Kachin, Kayah, Kayin, Chin, Bamar, Mon, Rakhine and Shan. According to the 1983 census, the Bamar accounted for 69 per cent of the total population. Myanmar, the country's official language, is spoken in every region, but all ethnic groups also have their own language or dialect. Almost 90 per cent of the population embraces Theravada Buddhism, while the remaining 10 per cent practise Christianity, Islam, Hinduism or Animism.

The country has seven states, Kachin, Kayah, Kayin, Chin, Mon, Rakhine and Shan, as well as seven divisions, including Yangon, Mandalay, Ayeyarwady, Bago, Magwe, Sagaing and Tanintharyi. The states and divisions are subdivided into a total of 324 townships, and 71.3 per cent of the population live in rural areas.

5. Thailand

Thailand is bordered by Myanmar to the west, the Lao People's Democratic Republic to the north-east, Cambodia to the east, and Malaysia to the south. It has a land area of 514,000 sq km and a population nearing 60 million, of whom more than 6 million live in its capital city, Bangkok. Ethnically, the population is made up of 80 per cent Thais, 15 per cent Chinese and 4 per cent Malays. The predominant religion in Thailand is Buddhism, although all other major religions are embraced in the country, including Christianity, Islam and Hinduism.

Thailand became a constitutional monarchy in 1932 when a parliamentary political system was established, replacing absolute monarchy. Over the ensuing 60 years, democracy developed gradually in the country as a result of frequent military coup d'etats and short-lived governments.

Thailand's economy was traditionally agriculture-based, and rice was its major export product. The country is still the world's leading producer of rice, but manufactured goods have now replaced rice as the major foreign exchange earner.

Economic development has brought major gains to the country. Real GDP per capita climbed from US$ 985 in 1960 to US$ 7,742 in 1995. Quality medical services are now available throughout most of the remote areas of the country. The infant mortality rate decreased from 103 to 31 per 1,000 live births from 1960 to 1996, while life expectancy increased by 17 years in the same period.

In the education sector, the adult literacy rate increased from 78 per cent in 1970 to 94 per cent in 1995. Sex-desegregated data show that the literacy rate for women is lower than that for men, at 91.6

per cent as compared with 96 per cent, which reflects the gender roles of past generations. Today, equal numbers of girls and boys are enrolled in school, but Thailand still has low school enrolment rates, particularly at the secondary school level.

Alongside the positive changes, numerous problems have also emerged over the past four development decades, including severe environmental degradation such as deforestation; water pollution resulting from untreated industrial waste; and air pollution exceeding critical levels in Bangkok. Income levels have increased throughout the country, but so too have income disparities between rich and poor people. Rural-to-urban migration, particularly from the north-east to Bangkok and its surrounding provinces, has been tremendous because of highly centralized industrial development policies. However, the quality of life of migrants has been low, owing to poor working and living conditions.

In July 1997, Thailand was hit by a financial crisis, which sent its economy into recession. Unemployment has soared since that time and underemployment is rife. The economic crisis has affected children particularly hard, with dropout rates increasing and family problems on the rise. Government education, health and employment programmes have all been affected. However, Thailand has shown signs of an improved economy and is making modest progress in tackling some of these related social problems.

6. Viet Nam

Viet Nam is situated on the Indochinese peninsula. The country's land area is 330,991.5 sq km. It has 3,451 km of coastline and land borders of 1,555 km with the Lao People's Democratic Republic, 1,281 km with China and 982 km with Cambodia. In administrative management, the country is divided into 61 provinces. The largest city is Ho Chi Minh City, followed by Hanoi, Haiphong and Danang.

In 1996, the population of Viet Nam reached 75 million, making it the twelfth most populous country in the world. Eighty-four per cent of the population is ethnic Vietnamese, two per cent ethnic Chinese and the rest are Khmers, Chams and members of some 60 ethno-linguistic groups. Four philosophies and religions have shaped the spiritual life of the Vietnamese people, namely, Confucianism, Taoism, Christianity and Buddhism, but Buddhism is the predominant religion in the country.

24

According to a census taken in 1994, only 20 per cent of Vietnamese people live in urban centres and 80 per cent of their livelihood is agrarian, even though cultivated land accounts for only 20 per cent of the total surface of the country. The remaining land consists of hills, mountains, highlands and forests.

Viet Nam is one of the poorest countries in Asia, with an estimated per capita income of less than US$ 300 per year, while the population growth rate is 2.2 per cent, above the average growth rate of the world, especially among ethnic minorities (about 13 per cent of the total population). The living conditions for most Vietnamese are very difficult. According to the General Statistics Office, 20 per cent of the population live under the poverty line (countryside 22 per cent; town 10 per cent). Twenty-four per cent of babies born weigh no more than 2.5 kg at birth. Education and health care are limited in scope and service. According to an evaluation carried out by ADB, Viet Nam has a large public medical network but, owing to economic difficulties, medical resources and facilities are decreasing seriously, especially in the remote regions of the country.

The Vietnamese agricultural industry has been growing incrementally in the last decade. The year 1997 marked the highest increase ever. According to the government report from the second session of the Tenth National Assembly, Viet Nam produced 30.6 million tons of food in 1997, an increase of 1.4 million tons as compared with 1996. Food production has had a high rate of development, averaging an increase of 5.6 per cent (1.29 million tons) yearly. This is the highest increase level in Asian countries (1.8 per cent) as well as in the world (1.7 per cent). The average yearly food output now stands at 400 kg for each Vietnamese, whereas in 1975 it was 240.6 kg, and in 1987, 280.8 kg.

In recent years, Viet Nam has opened its doors to the world market. There have been both advantages and disadvantages to this current economic change. On the positive side, the new market economy has brought many new business opportunities for Viet Nam to expand its industries and markets, and thus its gross national production and income. However, interaction with the outside world has brought some negative side effects and many new challenges, including in the areas of employment, education and health. In addition, the gap between rich and poor and between different regions is increasing rapidly.

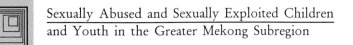

Along with economic and demographic changes, the market economy has had a negative influence on the social and cultural life of the Vietnamese people. It is important to note, however, that sexual abuse and sexual exploitation are not new social problems in Viet Nam. These abuses against children existed prior to the market based economy, as in many other nations. However, the recent industrialization and modernization of Viet Nam have increased these problems to the point where they have become a national concern.

Chapter III

Methodology

The project design is based on an interactive process whereby the children and social service and health-care providers are informants of the research. Given the nature of the data to be collected and the subjects, the researchers used qualitative research approaches. The project began with an initial planning phase when the research methodology was developed, teams were identified and trained in research methods. This was followed by an exploratory phase, in which primary data on the background and locations of the children, their health problems and their care-seeking behaviour in all six countries were collected and analysed by the research teams. Information was also collected on the nature of the services available to sexually abused and sexually exploited children and the capabilities of the staff to provide care.

These planning and exploratory phases enabled the research team to be familiar with and initiate discussions with children, communities and service providers. The information on the agencies and their programmes was vital for establishing potential collaborators in the field and the gaps in their current programmes. Interventions on awareness-raising at the community level were designed based on the findings of the research. The pilot projects were developed at national HRD workshops held in each of the participating countries for social and health-care providers, and are currently being implemented by the national coordinating organizations in each of the six countries. Apart from developing the pilot projects, the workshop participants also discussed the research findings and analysed their training needs. Specific interventions for the effective delivery of care to the victims and potential victims of sexual abuse and sexual exploitation will be designed by the national coordinating organizations during the ESCAP subregional course for 30 social service and health-care providers from the subregion, which is scheduled for September 2000. The follow-up projects will be implemented over an eight-month period following the course, and thereafter evaluated at a national seminar in each of the six countries. The following section covers the planning and exploratory phases of the project.[3]

A. PLANNING PHASE

1. Adaptation of the research methodology

Researchers working with children in exceptionally difficult circumstances have noted that surveys and quantitative research approaches often fail to generate valid data. This research, therefore, utilized a qualitative research methodology that has been developed by the expert on the subject, Wanjiku Kaime-Atterhog, and used among children in prostitution in Thailand and street children in Kenya. A key aspect of this method is the understanding that children and care providers are knowledgeable of their own "world" and researchers can only really understand these "worlds" by listening to and learning from their respondents. Furthermore, any interventions for these two target groups aimed at improving their situation must be based on such an understanding if it is to have any meaningful impact on their lives.

In order to provide guidance to the country research teams, a detailed set of methodology notes was produced, as well as a research protocol.[4] A broadly qualitative and participative approach was set out in which the following were the main methods used:

- Review of documentary and archival information, including reports, evaluations, registers, videos etc.;

- Observation of programme activities, adopting participant observation techniques where appropriate;

- Informal discussions with a wide variety of people encountered during visits of observation; and

- Semi-structured interviews with sexually abused and sexually exploited children and youth, programme managers, medical staff, social staff, teachers etc.

---

[3] Detailed information on the intervention phase can be obtained from the ESCAP HRD web site < www.escap-hrd.org >.

[4] See the interview guide in annex II.

2. Selection and training
of the national research teams

Owing to the sensitivity of the topics under investigation and the sustainability of the project, it was proposed that local staff members from the national coordinating organizations conduct the research. Many government officers, however, are responsible for developing and implementing policies and programmes on sexual abuse and sexual exploitation of children and youth in their respective countries, often without an understanding of the real problems and needs of the target groups. This therefore involved identifying appropriate persons from the national coordinating organizations that had some previous experience in participative research or were working with young people and had an interest in research.

In two countries, China and Thailand, the national coordinating bodies lacked the staff to carry out the research and, together with ESCAP, identified local academic institutions to serve as the national research focal points. In Myanmar, the government officers worked alongside staff from the psychology department and did not entirely hand over the research activities to an academic institution. These national research teams were then trained on sampling and data collection methods and techniques by ESCAP, but it is to the credit of the national research teams that the research generated a large amount of rich data.

The researchers came from a wide range of different academic and professional backgrounds, which undoubtedly enriched the material that they generated. Research sites were also selected during the research methods training sessions based on the following criteria: the provinces should be rural and urban centres known to have a large number of children engaged in prostitution and sexually abused children; and the provinces should be those that serve as areas of origin, transit and destination for children who are trafficked within or outside the country for purposes of prostitution. The research teams then decided on the specific districts that they would target for the study.

More specifically, the research teams were trained in sampling methods and techniques to establish trust and friendship with the children and care providers. Because of the difficulties involved in identifying sexually abused and sexually exploited children and service providers, the researchers were familiarized with the snowball sampling method. This method begins the interview process with a few interviewees and then relies on them to expand the contacts. In order to avoid bias in identifying the target groups to be interviewed, the researchers were asked to consult other sources of information in the community. Various methods were explored in the training work-shops to access children at highly concealed places of work such as brothels. These included such methods as collaboration with health workers in the area who were already involved in care provision to the target group, police officers, or posing as clients or pimps.

Research teams employing such undercover techniques were requested always to reveal their true identity and purpose to the children and obtain their consent before conducting the interviews. Unfortunately, some country teams did not reveal their identity or objectives of the research to the children they interviewed in brothels. Adequate sample size, utilizing the snowball method, is obtained when the data from the samples consistently repeat themselves and reveal definite patterns of information. The data that are obtained from such a sample are reliable in explaining behavioural patterns.

To establish trust, the research teams were asked to begin with observational and informal interviews selecting a topic of interest and one easy to discuss before moving to in-depth interviews. Once a relationship was developed, the researchers used a semi-structured interview procedure to guide their discussions, relying heavily on the spontaneous generation of questions as they emerge naturally from the free-flowing discussion between them and the respondent. Moreover, they were asked to make use of the immediate surroundings to increase the relevancy, concreteness and immediacy of interview questions and responses. The research teams were also encouraged to help children, especially those who might have appeared to be traumatized by talking about their abusive and exploitative experiences, whenever they could, including providing basic counselling, or refer-ring them to counsellors. However, there were few cases in which the researchers intervened in order to assist the children. One example is of a girl interviewed in Khammouane Province in Lao People's Democratic Republic, who had been working in a local pub for two weeks. She had not been sexually exploited but she was homesick and wanted to go back to live with her parents a long way from town. She had no money or knowledge about how to return because she had been accompanied by relatives who had left her at the pub to earn money. The researchers thought she was at high risk of being sexually exploited and so they sent her home on a bus.

Owing to the sensitivity of the information to be collected from the children and service providers, and the importance of keeping the interviewing environment as natural as possible, the research teams were requested not to use a tape recorder at the beginning, but to do so at a later stage, once trust had been established. Regretfully, some national research teams used concealed tape recorders without the consent of the children.

The training also focused on methods of recording and analysing data obtained from observations and interviews.

The national research teams from the six participating countries comprised the following persons.

In **Cambodia**, ESCAP selected the Cambodian Centre for the Protection of Children's Rights (CCPCR) to serve as the research focal point. The research team in Cambodia consisted of three staff members of CCPCR in Phnom Penh. The research team targeted nine provinces for the study, Koh Kong, Sihanoukville, Siem Riap, Kompong Chhnang, Phnom Penh, Kompong Cham, Poipet, Battambang and Svay Rieng. On average, the researchers spent 5 to 10 days at each research site and the data collection phase ran from April to June 1999.

In **China**, the All-China Youth Federation was chosen by ESCAP as the focal point for this project. The Yunnan Academy of Social Sciences was then designated as the research focal point. The fieldwork was conducted in Kunming, Quijing, Xishuangbanna and Hekou. The research team comprised six staff members of the Academy who split into two groups to collect the data. The research was conducted from October to December 1998, with staff spending one to two weeks in each research site.

In **the Lao People's Democratic Republic**, the Department of Social Welfare under the Ministry of Labour and Social Welfare served as the national focal point for this project. The Deputy Director of the Social Welfare Department was the coordinator of the project. The research team consisted of staff of the Department of Social Welfare from the Ministry and Vientiane Municipality and from the Lao People's Revolutionary Youth Union. The fieldwork was carried out from June to July 1998 and the researchers spent 15 days in each province.

The Department of Social Welfare served as the national focal point for this project in **Myanmar**. A professor of the Psychology Department, Yangon University, coordinated the research. The research team members comprised people from the Psychology Department of Yangon University, the Department of Social Welfare and the Rehabilitation Centre for Ex-Drug Addicts. Two research teams carried out fieldwork simultaneously owing to unavoidable delays in the conduct of the study. The first team, Team A, was assigned to conduct fieldwork in Muse, which is situated on the Myanmar-China border, and Yangon. The second team, Team B, was assigned to conduct the study in Hpa-an and Mawlamyine, which are situated in the southern part of the country.

In **Thailand**, the National Commission on Women's Affairs initially served as the national focal point for this project. (The focal point was changed to the National Youth Bureau in mid-1999). The research focal point was Chulalongkorn University and a child psychiatrist at the University served as the research coordinator. The research team members comprised staff of the University, child psychiatrists from Vajira and Ramathibodhi hospitals, and a nurse and volunteer from the Centre for the Protection of Children's Rights Bangkok. The data were collected from the provinces of Chiang Mai, Chiang Rai, Nakhon Ratchasima, Udon Thani, Khon Kaen, Nakhon Pathom, Bangkok, Rayong, Chonburi, Songkhla, Phuket and Trang from October 1997 to May 1998.

The Department of Social Evils Prevention served as the national focal point for the project in **Viet Nam**. The Department organized a research group including eight of its own specialists and researchers from the Institute of Labor Science and Social Affairs and the Centre for Human and Labor Resources (both under Ministry of Labour, Invalids and Social Affairs). In order to complete the project in three months and within the proposed budget, the team was divided into two groups. Team A worked in Hanoi and Lang Son provinces and Team B in Danang, Khanh Hoa, Ho Chi Minh City and Can Tho.

B. EXPLORATORY PHASE

1. Preparation for fieldwork

The research teams in all six countries began by locating and reviewing available documents, including medical and police records, and studies conducted by international organizations and governmental institutions on sexually abused and sexually exploited children. The data were reviewed and summarized to provide an overview of the areas where sexual abuse and sexual exploitation were prevalent, and the organizations that worked with the victims and potential victims in the respective coutries. The research team members also held discussions with care providers in organizations providing services to sexually abused and sexually exploited children to obtain information on the research sites and interviewees.

In Viet Nam, for example, the Department of Social Evils Prevention wrote to the provincial branches of the Ministry of Labour, Invalids and Social Affairs in all the six research sites requesting information on sexually abused and sexually exploited children and youth and available services. In Thailand, where the national research team comprised medical professionals, information was sought from hospitals and other health-care facilities, including the Division of Venereal Diseases Control. The Centre for the Protection of Children's Rights, where one of the team members worked as a volunteer, was also visited. The team in Myanmar held preparatory meetings to review the objectives of the research, identify research sites, distribute and discuss the interview guides and to develop a detailed programme for the two teams. In the Lao People's Democratic Republic, the research teams compiled their own lists of questions based on the interview guides. In order to conduct a research project in the Lao People's Democratic Republic, government cooperation is necessary at all levels. Thus, the next step was to obtain permission from the Minister of Labour and Social Welfare. After the permission had been obtained the researchers divided themselves into two research teams. In China, the Yunnan Academy of Social Sciences interviewed all the different departments concerned, such as public security and health, before conducting the fieldwork. Owing to the sensitive nature of the issues, they integrated in-depth interviews with the question-naires. In addition, group discussions were held.

The last step before primary data collection was the translation of all the interview guides into the six local languages.

2. Community entry phase: establishing a presence

At the provincial level, researchers made initial contact with social welfare offices, police and some NGOs to brief them on the project and its purpose as well as to collect general information on the situation of sexually abused and sexually exploited children in the province.

In Cambodia, the research teams contacted the Commissar of the provincial and municipal police headquarters to ensure some level of security for the team members should it be required. In addition, researchers met with relevant sections of the Ministry of Social Action and Veteran Affairs, district police inspectors and some NGOs in the province, which were working with sexually abused and sexually exploited children, in order to obtain more information about the problem. In the Lao People's Democratic Republic, the provincial

officers introduced the researchers to officials at the provincial govern-
ing office. There they met with representatives of the Lao Youth
Union, the Lao Women's Union and the police to obtain information
on the situation of the children concerned at each research site. After
the provincial-level meetings, researchers were accompanied by officers
from the Ministry of Labour and Social Welfare and introduced to
district-level police officials who were able to provide area-specific
information regarding location and methods for contacting such
children. In China, the researchers interviewed government departments at each research site. In Viet Nam, the researchers worked with
the provincial branches of the Ministry of Labour, Invalids and Social
Affairs, and the Committee for the Care and Protection of Children in
each province. The research team also requested the assistance of
officials from the Viet Nam Women's Union and the police in the field.

3. Identification and selection of target groups

Sexually abused and sexually exploited children and youth are
sensitive issues in all countries and areas of the subregion and the
researchers used several methods to locate them as well as their
caregivers. In Cambodia, for example, the researchers spent time
surveying the brothel areas prior to selecting their entry strategy and
tried to target both open and closed brothels for their interviews in
each province. The male researchers posed as clients, while the female
researchers posed as pimps or brothel owners. In some instances, the
researcher also disguised herself as a man in order to enter closed
brothels. In this way, they were able to identify and interview 65
children, including 55 girls and 10 boys. More time would have been
required for the researcher to build up trust with the boys and to
gather their full stories.

In the Lao People's Democratic Republic, as another example, the
researchers identified sexually exploited children from police files as
well as from the children's friends. The local police officers also
tipped them about entertainment establishments where children were
known to be engaged in prostitution, and even accompanied them to
those entertainment places. The researchers initially made enquiries
with the establishment owners and the friends and relatives of sexually
abused children about the location and backgrounds of the children.
Using this approach, they were able to identify and interview 43 girls
who were sexually exploited. Although researchers identified children
who had been sexually abused from police records, they decided it was
inappropriate to interview them as the situations seemed to have been
resolved and they did not want to upset the children by asking them

to recount their stories. The researchers also interviewed doctors in two clinics and two hospitals, a secondary school teacher, representatives of the Lao Women's Union and the Lao Youth Union, and a pharmacist.

4. Methods of data collection

Data were collected through observation, in-depth interviews and group discussions. Techniques to establish trust and friendship with the children were emphasized during all of the interviews in the participating countries. In **Cambodia**, the three researchers differed in their approach. One researcher tried to take the children he interviewed away from the others, either by taking the girl into her room or by leading her away from the brothel. He took the time to explain the purpose of the study to the girls whom he interviewed and he built up the girl's trust in him through conversation. Another researcher always interviewed the girl in open areas within the brothel while simultaneously engaging in other activities that the girls enjoyed, including playing cards, singing, watching television and eating. He felt that conducting the interview in that informal way made the girl feel at ease. In addition, a female researcher spoke about her own life or pretended that she knew the girl's parents in order to secure the trust of the children. Two of the researchers never revealed their true identity as they felt they lacked the time needed to explain the objectives of the study to the girls. Furthermore, they feared that the girls would reveal their identity to the brothel owner, which might have endangered them. Most of the interviews lasted from half an hour to two hours. In some cases, when more information was required, the researchers returned to the brothel for a second interview. All researchers taped interviews using small concealed cassette recorders, and following the interviews recorded information and observations on paper.

The research teams from **Yunnan Province (China)** conducted in-depth interviews and had the children fill out questionnaires. In addition, group discussions were held. The researchers used tape recorders and transcribed the interviews later. Working with the local women's federations, they were able to locate the girls for interviewing, and conduct on-the-spot investigations. The researchers also spent much time observing the environment before the interview, to better acquaint themselves with the girls' situation. It was often necessary to provide detailed assurances to the children that they would be treated with respect in the interviews and that the researchers would not expose them and damage their reputation.

In Savannakhet and Khammouane provinces in **the Lao People's Democratic Republic**, the girls felt more comfortable speaking to a woman researcher. Interviews were usually conducted with individual children but in some places it was necessary to meet with two or three children. For some interviews, conducted in Khammouane and Savannakhet, researchers brought the children together in a larger group of five or six children for a meal and an informal discussion. After the meal, the researcher interviewed the children separately. During the interviews, she asked questions while another researcher took notes. In Vientiane Municipality and Champasack Province, the two male team members posed as clients in order to collect data from the sexually exploited children. They did this after they realized from the first few interviews that the children were reluctant to talk to them. The researchers suspected that the children might have thought they were police officers who wanted to arrest them, or the girls might have felt uncomfortable talking with men about their situation. In these cases, it was necessary to interview the children first, and write down their answers later.

The research teams from **Myanmar** conducted the interviews in quiet places with no interruptions. They used tape recorders, with the children's permission, to record interviews that lasted for one hour to three hours. The researchers also kept a daily diary, including verbal and expressive material from each child.

In **Thailand**, where most of the research team members were psychiatrists, a psychiatric assessment was conducted together with the semi-structured interview of each child. Brief, focused counselling was provided to children when required and relevant. Observation of health-care facilities, correction homes and centres that were visited was also carried out. When possible, group discussions were conducted with children, care providers and local people in order to obtain a more thorough understanding of their feelings, attitudes and opinions on sexual abuse and sexual exploitation.

The researchers in **Viet Nam** made the children comfortable by having a local staff member who was acquainted with the families hold informal conversation. The research team members were introduced as social officers and not researchers. Once the families were relaxed, the researchers would slowly begin their interviews, beginning with general information. Members of the research team worked in pairs, with one person asking the questions and the other taking down notes. They also recorded the interviews, although this was not always with consent from the children. They felt that the families appeared comfortable with the team because they were in the company of officers known to them.

5. Methods of data analysis

The teams used tables based on the interview questions to facilitate data entry.   In those countries where tape recorders were used, the teams first transcribed the data and then coded them, examining common patterns of behaviour as well as variations.   Both question and content analysis methods were used to summarize and describe the data from each province in the participating countries. The provincial data were then analysed and synthesized to present a qualitative country assessment of the services and health needs of sexually abused and sexually exploited children in each country.   The reports from Cambodia, Viet Nam and Thailand were first written in the local languages and then translated into English by the team members.   The Yunnan Province (China), the Lao People's Democratic Republic and Myanmar reports were written in English.   The ESCAP team, working together with the research teams, produced more complete and thorough reports.

6. Problems encountered

The researchers encountered common problems in their study. They all felt that they lacked sufficient time both to establish trust with sexually abused and sexually exploited children and to conduct in-depth interviews.   Many of the researchers did not conduct interviews in the provinces with health-care providers, social workers and teachers owing to limited time and resources.   They did, however, interview managers of organizations providing services to the target group.

In **Cambodia**, the presence of armed guards and brothel owners in some cases hampered the interview process, as the girls were afraid to speak out.   Some researchers did not enter these brothels, themselves fearing the guards.   The research team also felt that they had lost some interview information owing to the secretive procedure followed, which did not allow for the manual recording of information at the time of the interview.

In **China**, the issues of sexual abuse and sexual exploitation are very sensitive.   It was thus necessary for the researchers to visit service providers once or twice to explain in detail the purpose of the project prior to conducting the interviews.   In addition, as prostitution is illegal in China, it was difficult for the children to admit that they were involved in illegal activities.   This made it difficult for the researchers to identify and approach the girls.   To deal with these problems, the researchers spent a considerable amount of time observing the girls before approaching them, and treated them with a respectful attitude.

The teams in **the Lao People's Democratic Republic** had problems finding sexually exploited children, as they are highly mobile. In several instances, when the researchers went to find the children who had been referred to them by the child's friend, a police officer, or another key informant, they were sometimes told that the girl had moved on to another pub or restaurant located in a different province or district. At times, the pub owners would not co-operate with the researchers or the police who accompanied them because they were afraid of being arrested or they were annoyed that the researchers were taking too much of the girl's time from customers who were spending money at the pub. To deal with this problem, the researchers bought drinks and food while they were conducting interviews or making observations. Researchers suspected that the children might have been lying about or did not know their ages. This may have been because prostitution is illegal.

For the male researchers it was often difficult to ask the girls about their sexual health. Thus, the researchers would spend time drinking soda or beer with the girls in order to put them at their ease. Further, when asking about condom usage, if the researchers were posing as customers, the girls might not have told the researchers about their true condom use behaviour. This could be because they would be more likely to tell a prospective customer what they would want to hear about previous condom usage rather than divulge their actual behaviour.

In **Myanmar**, many of the brothels where girls were known to be working were located across the borders and the researchers had no access to them.

As the researchers had extensive networks in the field, and employed local health professionals known to the children, no problems were encountered in **Thailand**.

Sexual abuse cases were especially difficult to identify and interview in many of the countries. In **Viet Nam**, most of the sexually abused children identified from police records came from families which had not received satisfactory compensation or those threatened by the sex offenders. Thus, the sample of sexually abused children represented a specific group of children. For children involved in prostitution, the researchers felt that the data collected were not precise, as the children were not consistent on a number of points. However, the researchers tried to control this by rephrasing the questions. Researchers also found that giving children toys, candy and various gifts helped in gaining their trust and acquiring more accurate information.

Chapter IV

Research Findings

A. SUBREGIONAL SYNTHESIS

A total of 84 sexually abused children and 176 sexually exploited children (27 of whom had a history of sexual abuse) were interviewed. The majority of these children were girls, most probably owing to the assumptions on the part of the national researchers that boys in their respective countries were neither sexually abused nor sexually exploited. The following is a brief subregional analysis of the findings, followed by national summaries. There is more information available from Thailand than from other countries as the researchers were medical professionals who had access to hospitals and existing data. Thus, the national summary for Thailand is more in-depth than the others. In addition, as each country research team wrote its report in a unique style, the national summaries in this chapter do not follow the same format. As the research was qualitative in nature, the country analysis reflects the specific situation and findings of the research reports, and cannot be generalized as the situation for all sexually abused and sexually exploited children.

1. Who are the children/youth?

The children and youth enduring sexual abuse and sexual exploitation were from both urban and rural areas but more of the sexual abuse cases tended to be from the countryside, while the sexual exploitation cases were mostly from urban areas. Children enduring sexual abuse were found to be younger; the majority were aged 6 to 12 years, and a few were under 6 years. Those children who had endured sexual exploitation were older and of pubescent age, between 13 and 17 years. Many of the children were born in poor peasant or working-class families. The children, as well as their parents, tended to have little formal education. Moreover, many of the children enduring sexual abuse and exploitation came from families with special conditions or dysfunctional families, for example, the parents were divorced, the mother or father had a second wife or husband, the parents were addicted to drugs, drank alcohol, and quarrelled frequently.

2. What are the causes?

(a) Sexual exploitation

The findings from all six countries indicate that illiteracy and low levels of education increase children's vulnerability to sexual exploitation. In the Lao People's Democratic Republic, for example, for several of the children and young women included in the study, the only available employment options were factory jobs where the working conditions were difficult and the salaries low. These factors motivated children to find lighter jobs in pubs, where they sold alcohol to customers and then gradually drifted into prostitution. Others were trafficked into prostitution through false promises of jobs as maids and helpers in the cities. These children were often sold to brothel owners and further fell victim to a vicious cycle of sexual exploitation and domination. Neglected children and youth were at higher risk of being cheated by traffickers. For some groups of children, such as the street children from Thailand, commercial sexual activities were the only way they could earn money to feed themselves. Most of the shelters for street children in Thailand were found to be ineffective as the children felt confined and thus preferred to live the "free" life on the streets. The Thailand study also found that caregivers in many of the organizations working with sexually abused and sexually exploited children lacked the knowledge and skills required to provide these children with appropriate care. Thus some of the sexually exploited children ran away from the social rehabilitation centres and returned to prostitution.

Past history of sexual abuse is another factor that was identified as contributing to the sexual exploitation of children and youth. The link between sexually abused children and sexually exploited children is that many children who are sexually abused become vulnerable to sexual exploitation because their societies ostracize them for losing their virginity. Customs, practices and censures ostracize them, which further renders them vulnerable to victimization. The family and social prestige overrides the safety and psychological well-being of the child.

Children in all the participating countries were found to lack adequate knowledge about health-related issues, including the health effects of sexual abuse and sexual exploitation. As a result, they were easily lured into prostitution. The studies in all countries also found that many children were not aware of the relevant laws that protected their rights. Many children also did not know what sexual abuse and sexual exploitation entailed and thus it was impossible for them to protect themselves. Furthermore, it was found that this was particularly prevalent among minority ethnic groups and in border areas that have proved difficult to target under past education and awareness-raising campaigns.

Another major cause of sexual exploitation seemed to be the family's economic situation: the families were poor and thus the children became major contributors to the family's income. As a consequence, such children often left their homes to go to town to earn money. Part of the earned money was sent back home to their family, and the other part was kept for their own subsistence. In addition, some parents of poor families sold their children to brothels or encouraged them to engage in prostitution. The Cambodia study found that parents who sold their children into prostitution did so out of ignorance and had no knowledge of the conditions of the brothels or the health effects of commercial sex work. In most cases, children respected their parents and other elders, and thus they followed their advice.

Except in China, the Lao People's Democratic Republic and Thailand where the majority of the children interviewed in the studies could enter prostitution "willingly" and could leave, children were forced by others or circumstances or cheated into prostitution. The studies showed that several members of the community were involved in the trafficking of children.

Rural poverty and rapid urban growth were identified as two key factors that contributed to children and youth's vulnerability to sexual exploitation. Lack of adequate facilities, including sports centres, in rural areas made children vulnerable to substance abuse and sexual exploitation, as they lacked opportunities to use their free time in a constructive way.

The studies also showed that in many countries, the police and military were involved in the prostitution and trafficking of children and youth. In some provinces in one country, these officers were the owners of sex establishments housing child prostitutes and profited from the sexual trafficking of children. Thus, few officials were actively involved in defending children against sexual exploitation or punishing perpetrators. Current laws in all countries, except Thailand, are not clearly defined and do not offer adequate protection for children against sexual abuse and sexual exploitation. Furthermore, the punishments stipulated in the current laws may not be severe enough to be commensurate with the subsequent harm to the child victims. Knowledge about such laws among the general population is also limited.

(b) Sexual abuse

In Myanmar and Thailand, biological factors were found to play a role in children's vulnerability to sexual abuse. Developmental disability prevented the children from defending themselves from the offender. In some severe cases, children were totally dependent on the offender. Children from dysfunctional families – where parents were unable to care for their children owing to divorce, separation, or abandonment, sexual abuse and substance abuse – were extremely vulnerable. In Thailand, the study found that 53 per cent of families of the interviewed children were addicted to alcohol and drugs, thereby reducing the ability of parents to care for their children and increasing the likelihood of sexual abuse by an intoxicated male guardian. Psychiatric illness in a family member resulted in neglect of the child in some cases and sexual abuse of the child in others. Economic problems in the family, forcing parents to work late at night and to leave the children unattended or under the care of a friend, neighbour or relative, and cramped living conditions, where children and adults shared the same sleeping quarters, increased the risk of sexual abuse. The school environment was also found, in the Thailand study, to contribute to children's vulnerability to sexual abuse.

Sexual offenders used trickery, force or threats to sexually abuse children. The sexual acts usually took place in the child's house or the offender's house. Only in a few cases did the abuse take place in a deserted location. The sexual offenders were often neighbours of the children's families living close by, family friends, acquaintances, including baby-sitters, and some were even blood relatives. A majority of the cases were often "solved" by paying compensation to the family of the child. Thus, few sexually abused children received rehabilitation care. Moreover, in Thailand, punitive but no rehabilitative measures exist to deal with sexual offenders who are either fined or jailed. These forms of punishment were found not to deter sexual abusers from repeating their crime.

The legal process for cases of sexually abused children is currently extremely lengthy, and was found to put the child victims at risk of further abuse. In many cases, the victim had to be present in the courtroom during the trial and thus relive the trauma.

3. What are the physical and psychosocial health effects?

In all six studies, sexual abuse and sexual exploitation were found to affect the health and development of the children and youth involved greatly. As the studies were cross-sectional, the information available is concentrated on the direct effects of sexual experiences rather than the circumstances leading to the abuse and exploitation or the long-term and intergenerational effects. The direct effects relate to respiratory tract, skin and sexually transmitted infections, physical injury from violence or sexual abuse, pregnancy, abortion, affective, personality and organic mental disorders.

In Cambodia, sexually exploited children were often locked in confined places in dark rooms with insufficient oxygen and proper sanitation, which led to skin infections. The Cambodia, Lao People's Democratic Republic and Myanmar studies found that children were largely ignorant of preventive measures against sexually transmitted diseases and often engaged in unprotected sexual activities with multiple sexual partners, took medicine not prescribed by a medical doctor and abused substances. Thus, they were highly vulnerable to drug addiction and to contracting STDs, including HIV/AIDS. Many of the children in all countries were found to suffer from sexually transmitted diseases, including gonorrhoea, syphilis and herpes simplex, and some were HIV-positive. Children in the six countries that were engaged in commercial sex also complained of general physical illness, such as abdominal pain, headaches, body aches, fever and colds, insomnia, and a general feeling of malaise. In Yunnan Province (China) and Viet Nam, the study findings indicated that physical illness was higher among rural sexually exploited children than among their counterparts in urban areas. The findings on sexually abused children from the Thailand research indicated that these children had similar physical health problems to those of sexually exploited children. In addition, the sexually abused children experienced the tearing of genitals, peptic ulcer, dizziness and hair fallout.

The psychosocial effects of children and youth subjected to sexual abuse and sexual exploitation are not easy to diagnose. Some of the common problems experienced by the children in the six countries include low self-esteem, symptoms of psychological stress, rejection from the families, stigmatization by societies, substance abuse, anger, shame, despair, disregard of any circumstances, insecurity, indecisiveness and restlessness. The Myanmar study found that some of the sexually abused and sexually exploited children preferred to stay alone, while others continually ran away from home. Sexually exploited children in the Myanmar study felt trapped, humiliated and insecure and lacked confidence.

Sexually exploited girls in the Lao People's Democratic Republic study had overly promiscuous behaviour, trauma, and depression. In Yunnan Province (China), the children experienced profound feelings of loneliness and self-blame. Moreover, the girls in the Lao People's Democratic Republic and China studies felt isolated and sad owing to their ostracization from families, relatives and communities and the lack of positive social support. The only social support that the girls received was from their girl friends who worked with them, and from the pub owners. Most of the sexually exploited children could not obtain family support because they were ashamed to tell their parents about their true work situation. Some parents knew of their work situation but did not know how to protect their children. The consequence of having no social support is isolation, which in turn often prevents the girls from seeking a way out of sexual exploitation.

The findings from the Cambodia study indicated that street children were addicted to cigarettes and glue sniffing to ward off hunger. Many of these children and youth had experienced physical abuse, which made them angry and aggressive. The sexually abused and sexually exploited children in the Cambodia study also felt angry and sad because they were betrayed by people they loved and trusted. They often felt homesick and wanted the company of their family and friends but were ashamed, which left them feeling helpless, depressed and, in extreme cases, they mutilated themselves or attempted suicide. Many children and youth from all the six countries indicated that they would leave the commercial sex industry if they were provided with alternative means of earning an income.

In Thailand, sexually abused children were found to have many of the above-mentioned psychosocial manifestations as well as nail-biting, epilepsy and seizure from tension caused by the traumatic experience and stressful changes such as moving away from home, changing schools, adjusting to living in a Home, and living with the knowledge that the abuser was still at large. The researchers also noted that sexually abused children and youth who were interviewed soon after the sexual abuse had taken place showed signs of fear, anxiety and depression, while those who were interviewed several months after the abuse had taken place showed signs of anger, aggressiveness and inappropriate behaviour. Additional emotional problems included irritability, hopelessness, daydreaming, re-experiencing the abuse, tearfulness and loneliness. Sexually abused children and youth in the Thailand study also slashed their wrists and cut themselves and attempted suicide, including jumping from a building, igniting the bedroom, overdosing on sleeping pills, and toxic substance intoxication. Several of the children were also found to abuse substances.

The Viet Nam study showed that the greatest aspiration of sexually abused children, along with that of their families, was the severe punishment of the sexual offenders. At the same time, these children wanted their violation kept secret by authorities so that their future happiness would not be influenced.

4. What services are available to the children?

At present, no specific, tailored organizations exist in **Yunnan Province (China), the Lao People's Democratic Republic** and **Myanmar** to assist sexually abused children and sexually exploited children, and no health-care professionals or social workers are well trained in handling cases of sexually abused and sexually exploited children. Social and health services in the rural areas are particularly scant. The mainstream medical services that could cater for these children are not well publicized and thus are not sufficiently used.

In **Viet Nam,** the research indicated that, although organizations existed in the different provinces to work with children who had been sexually abused or sexually exploited, there were still not enough organizations working with these children, especially since this type of organization was established at most five years ago. Furthermore, though a number of such organizations, both national and international, may exist in large urban centres such as Ho Chi Minh City, this is not the case in rural areas and border regions. In addition, owing to the large workload faced by the caregivers working in these organizations, it has been difficult for them to strengthen organizational networks, coordinate their activities and exchange information between the different agencies.

In **Thailand,** most of the Centres and Homes in the country are located in Bangkok and the central region and there is a lack of services in other provinces. Many of the existing organizations which serve sexually abused and sexually exploited children conduct emergency work and lack the capacity to carry out effective rehabilitation. The physical needs of these children who arrive at hospitals or emergency homes following their traumatic experiences are treated but they are often not rehabilitated. Community members refer several cases of sexually abused children to Bangkok, even when services are available in the province where the children live, owing to the lack of awareness of services. Many people, including health professionals, believe that if a child has no physical injuries, there is no need for therapy or rehabilitation. Children confide in teachers more than any other community member outside of their family members, but teachers are often not trained to assist these children effectively. In Thailand, boys are increasingly experiencing sexual abuse and sexual exploitation, but often do not seek care. Boys are less frequently rehabilitated as compared to girls, although the psychiatric trauma they undergo is just as severe.

In **Cambodia,** the study showed that public services that meet the basic human needs of the people are severely lacking. Literacy rates and school enrolment are low, especially among women and girls. Health-care facilities and resources, including medicine, are inaccessible to the overwhelming majority of the population. Health services for children and youth are particularly lacking. Insufficient income-earning job alternatives are available for children in Cambodia. Although some NGOs provide skills training and literacy services for children, these services are insufficient in number and do not span all provinces of the country. Moreover, they tend to target girls who have already been sexually exploited and not those who are at high risk of sexual exploitation. Employment creation for these girls, once trained, is also lacking. The study showed that few centres exist in Cambodia, which target the health needs of sexually abused and sexually exploited children. Most government centres that provide services to children do not target these children directly and they do not have the capacity to address their needs.

The research showed that most sexually exploited children are not in contact with health personnel and that an overwhelming majority of the children treated illnesses at the local pharmacy. Most of the children do not visit medical facilities owing to embarrassment, and the treatment they receive from pharmacies is inadequate.

B. COUNTRY SUMMARIES

1. Cambodia

Fifty-four sexually exploited children and three sexually abused children were interviewed in this study. Of the 54 sexually exploited children, eight had a history of sexual abuse. One of the sexually exploited children and one of the sexually abused children were boys and the rest were girls. Three of the children were under 15 years old and the youngest girl interviewed, working in Phnom Penh, was aged 12 years. With the exception of one girl, all of the children were single. Ninety-three per cent of the children interviewed Khmer and the remainder ethnically Vietnamese.

(a) Causes of sexual exploitation

Common patterns were discerned in the life experiences of the 54 sexually exploited children interviewed in this study, which offer insight into the causes of the sexual exploitation of children. The first characteristic, which the 53 sexually abused girls shared, was that they all performed the role of a provider in the family, but their incomes were minimal and insufficient. Strikingly, 71 per cent of the girls were the eldest children, while 20 per cent were the second oldest children. Another common feature among the girls was that they all shared the traditional belief that non-virgin single women were unfit to marry, even if their virginity was lost as result of sexual abuse. They saw prostitution as the primary employment choice for those women.

In addition to the gender roles and traditional beliefs upheld by the 53 girls, all of the girls experienced stressors in their family environment, which made them vulnerable to sexual exploitation. One of these stressors included the death or illness of one or both parents, which reduced family income as well as incurring funeral or medical costs. Half of the girls came from single-parent or orphaned families, which exacerbated the situation. With no social support system from the government to assist poor families and the shattering of extended family structures during the genocide years, the children were desperate to find employment to help their families.

Another stressor was famine. As most of the children originated from farming and fishing families, who depended on natural resources for their livelihood, environmental disasters made families extremely vulnerable.

Other stressors included physical abuse and sexual abuse. Children who were physically abused wished to leave their homes in order to escape the violence. Sexually abused girls left their homes out of shame. Of the 11 sexually abused children, 8 entered prostitution of their own accord owing to the belief that they had no other options.

Once the children were vulnerable to sexual exploitation, several contributing factors influenced their entry into prostitution. One common factor was ignorance on the part of the children. Seventy-two per cent of the girls were tricked by persons who offered them other forms of employment. One cause of this ignorance was low levels of education. Forty-seven per cent of the girls were illiterate and had never attended school. The remainder had completed up to six years of education and only one girl had finished Grade 8. Poverty was sited by 91 per cent of those interviewed as the primary reason for not attending school or for dropping out. The low levels of education among children were also indicative of a lack of skills with which to earn a sufficient income.

A second contributing factor was the ignorance of parents about the trafficking of children and about the lives of sexually exploited children. Illiteracy rates among the fathers and mothers of the children were 42 and 52 per cent respectively. Mothers had received substantially less education than fathers, with 11 per cent of mothers having completed between 6 and 12 years of education, as compared with 43 per cent of fathers. Although some parents sold their daughters into prostitution, many did not know the conditions of the brothels or the health risks involved with commercial sex work.

A third factor which facilitated the entry of the girls into prostitution was the presence of traffickers. Aside from the professionals, many girls were trafficked by people they trusted, such as boyfriends, neighbours and even family members. The high price paid for virgins by brothel owners, as well as the location of sex establishments, were common knowledge and thus many people profited from the lucrative business.

Lastly, the study showed that law enforcers did not enforce existing laws to protect children but instead they themselves abused the laws. In many provinces, policemen and soldiers owned brothels or protected brothels with their men.

(b) Factors affecting physical and psychosocial health

The living conditions of the sexually exploited children in the brothels were poor. Most of the girls lived in small, dark rooms lacking sufficient oxygen and proper sanitation facilities, which resulted in skin infections. The children led restricted lives and were often forced to remain in confined spaces, sometimes protected by armed guards.

Most of the children interviewed suffered from undernourishment and sleep deprivation. Fifty-seven per cent of the sexually exploited children were forced to sleep with one to five customers a day while another 37 per cent served 6 to 10 customers every day. In two cases, the children received more than 10 customers a day. Of the 53 sexually exploited girls, 45 had been subject to physical abuse at the hands of brothel owners and customers, the most common forms being hitting and kicking. Three girls were regularly whipped with electric wires. This physical abuse resulted in behavioural problems in the girls, including anger and aggression.

The most serious medical problems that the girls suffered were STDs, including HIV/AIDS. Nineteen of the 53 girls had STDs, including gonorrhoea, syphilis, herpes simplex, urinary tract infections and polyps, and six girls had contracted the AIDS virus. The sexually exploited children did not always use condoms, especially when they slept with their sweethearts. Also when a client was drunk, the child had even less control over his/her behaviour.

None of the girls were substance abusers while the boys were addicted to smoking and glue-sniffing to ward off hunger. The overwhelming majority of sexually exploited children treated their physical ailments at the local pharmacy owing to cost-effectiveness and accessibility. The girls only visited a doctor in extreme cases of illness.

The psychological difficulties faced by the young women resulted from several factors. Many of the girls were deceived by people whom they loved and trusted, and thus they felt betrayed, angry and sad. Most of the girls were homesick and wished to return home to the company of their family and friends but were too ashamed to do so and felt hopeless. In extreme cases of depression, some of the girls had attempted suicide and self-mutilation.

The overwhelming majority of the girls interviewed sought counsel from their friends when they encountered stressful periods. Those girls who lived in the brothel and the boys who lived on the street received no support from family, the community or NGOs.

Although 72 per cent of the girls interviewed aspired to become businesswomen, none of them had had access to non-formal education, including income-generating skills or vocational skills training.

(c) Available services/gaps in services

Services to address the physical and psychosocial needs of sexually abused and sexually exploited children in Cambodia were greatly lacking. One of the province studied, Poipet, had no services for children whatsoever. In two other provinces, Koh Kong and Kompong Chhnang, only a poorly serviced government orphanage existed which provided shelter for children but lacked adequate facilities and resources. None of the staff in those orphanages were trained to deal with sexually abused and sexually exploited children.

Sihanoukville, Svay Rieng and Battambang had NGOs with services for these children to meet their basic needs as well as to provide them with skills training, medical care and counselling services. The organizations also had reintegration programmes for the children.

In Siem Riap, an NGO provided much the same services as those in Sihanoukville, Svay Rieng and Battambang although in contrast street children were targeted and not sexually abused and sexually exploited children in particular. Street children are, however, vulnerable to both sexual abuse and sexual exploitation.

The majority of services which exist in Cambodia to assist such children are located in Phnom Penh. Six organizations run comprehensive programmes for these children, while another six run similar programmes targeted at street children.

(d) Case studies of government services

In Sihanoukville, the Provincial Orphanage of the Ministry of Social Action which houses 280 orphans and poor children, is supported by Association de Parrainage d'Enfants au Cambodge Viet Nam, Laos et Philippines (ASPECA) and the Assembly of God. The orphanage meets the basic needs of children and offers them literacy and vocational training classes. As yet, no specific programme exists to address the needs of sexually abused and sexually exploited children at the orphanage, although the Cambodian Centre for the Protection of Children's Rights has been trying to initiate such a response.

In Siem Riap, the Provincial Orphanage of the Ministry of Social Action provides services for children, although not specifically for sexually abused and sexually exploited children. Housing and food are provided to parentless and destitute children. The centre lacks resources and thus the quality of food, clothing and care, including medical care, is poor.

Kompong Chhnang has one orphanage run by the Ministry of Social Action and supported by ASPECA and the World Food Programme. At present, the orphanage cares for 26 children who are at high risk of sexual abuse and sexual exploitation. All of the children are very poor and some have been abandoned or orphaned. Many were living on the street before entering the orphanage.

The quantity and quality of services provided by the orphanage are poor. Children are given food and accommodation, but the orphanage suffers from a water shortage and the sleeping quarters lack sufficient oxygen. Many of the children have health problems owing to unsanitary conditions. The orphanage lacks the means to provide adequate medical and psychological support to the children.

Svay Rieng Province has one orphanage run by the Ministry of Social Action, which is currently supported by ASPECA. The orphanage caters for poor children, some of whom have been abandoned or orphaned. The orphanage meets the basic needs of children, including schooling, vocational training, clothing and food, but the quantity and quality of the services provided is poor owing to the small operational budget. The orphanage lacks the means to provide adequate medical and psychological support to the children. If the orphanage were to provide specific services for sexually abused and sexually exploited children, staff training and material resources would be required to address their needs.

Kompong Cham has one orphanage run by the Ministry of Social Action, which provides food and shelter to orphans, unaccompanied minors and disabled children. The services provided by the centre are highly inadequate. There are no government programmes in Battambang and Phnom Penh and no services, government or NGO, exist in Poipet to address the needs of children in especially difficult circumstances in general and sexually abused and sexually exploited children in particular.

(e) A case study of a sexually exploited child

Ny, a 17-year-old girl, lived at home with her parents and five siblings in Takeo Province. She left school after Grade 3 to work as a market seller. As the second eldest child of her poor family, Ny was eager to help her parents financially. When another seller in the market asked Ny to join her in a business in Koh Kong Province, Ny jumped at the chance of earning $US 20 per month.

After arriving in Koh Kong Province, Ny was locked in a hotel room for two days. She realized then that she had been deceived but had no way of escaping. On the third day, Ny's trafficker drugged her coffee, which left her semi-conscious and without any strength. A man was brought to the room and he raped her. The next day, Ny's fruitshake was drugged and another man raped her. The third day, Ny was raped when sober by yet another customer.

Following the third rape, Ny was set free. She went immediately to the police to file a complaint but they were disinterested in her testimony and did nothing to help her to return home. With no money, she decided to work as a bar girl to earn enough money to return home. She rented a room with some friends for a while but finally decided to live in a brothel as the rent of $US 50 per month consumed most of her earnings. At the time of the interview, Ny still lived in the brothel.

2. Yunnan Province (China)

Twenty-three girls who had been sexually exploited, as well as three sexually abused girls, were interviewed. Of the sexually exploited children, seven had previously been sexually abused. The majority of girls interviewed were between 17 and 24 years of age, but four of them had been trafficked between the ages of 14 to 18.

(a) Causes of sexual abuse and sexual exploitation

The research found that there were many contributing factors or stressors leading girls to enter the sex trade or to be trafficked. These factors included the pornographic establishments, traffickers taking advantage of ignorant children, changing moral attitudes among young people, gaps in economic development between regions, divorce of parents, lack of education among the girls as well as the family, prior sexual abuse, parental abandonment, lack of employment opportunities, and dissatisfaction in love affairs and marriage.

Only three sexually abused children were interviewed directly. These girls had all been abused by people known to them, such as their boyfriends, colleagues or male acquaintances. Only one of the girls had sought help after being abused, while the other two remained silent. This was because they knew that they would suffer humiliation if their abuse was made public. The girls confirmed that many cases were kept secret from the police, especially if it involved a family member.

Of the 23 sexually exploited children interviewed, 18 worked as pornographic attendants in a show business, where they paid money to the owner. The owners did not usually supply board and lodging for the girls, who had to pay their own expenses. The services they offered to clients ranged from person to person, and thus the price was adjusted accordingly. The girls all stated that it was difficult to leave the work because of the high income. Furthermore, the girls had all gradually reduced their communication with the outside world, and formed their own circle. This hindered their leaving commercial sex work.

Five girls interviewed had been trafficked and forced to sell their bodies because they had been ignorant and unaware of what to expect. Four of the girls had been trafficked to Thailand, where they were sold to the owner of a brothel at a high price. Another girl was trafficked to Thailand and then on to Malaysia, where she was forced to work in a brothel.

Two main reasons thus pushed girls into the commercial sex trade. The first concerned their individual experience. All the girls had strained relations with their parents, a low level of education, lack of employment opportunities and, for some girls, prior sexual abuse. The second set of reasons concerned their family and community life. The parents were often separated or divorced, had a low educational level, and were poor.

The educational level of the sexually exploited children who worked as pornographic attendants was generally higher than that of the girls trafficked into foreign countries and compelled to sell their bodies.

In addition, prior sexual abuse was a main stressor in causing girls to become children in prostitution. Seven of the 23 sexually exploited children interviewed had once been abused sexually, but none of them reported it to the police or sought any medical, psychological or social assistance. Because they thought they would lose face if they lost their chastity, they hushed up the scandal and bore the humiliation alone rather than tell their family members. It was very common for these girls to slip into the commercial sex trade once they felt frustrated in employment or marriage, or were influenced by friends.

(b) Factors affecting physical and psychosocial health

The majority of the sexually exploited children (the 18 girls who worked in pornographic establishments) had some knowledge of STDs and AIDS; however, there were many cases of STDs, pregnancy and gynaecological diseases among the 18 girls. Other than that, they were generally in good health.

Psychological problems included feelings of inferiority, self-blame, guilt, sadness, loneliness, tantrums, feelings of humiliation, feeling trapped, lack of self-confidence, a sense of floating and feelings of frustration and dejection.

The five girls who had been trafficked knew very little about STDs and AIDS. In addition, a great obstacle for them was reintegration into the community. They were looked down upon by their village, and had difficulty getting married. Two girls chose to marry people outside their village, while others remained unmarried. As these girls were often trafficked by their acquaintances and friends (even boyfriends), they had very strong feelings of being trapped and humiliated.

The three sexually abused children all appeared to be in good health. However, although they knew how to avoid becoming pregnant and used condoms with their boyfriends, pregnancy was common. The girls had many psychological problems. These included feelings of inferiority, self-blame, guilt, loneliness, tantrums, feelings of humiliation, sadness, feeling trapped, feelings of dejection, lack of self-confidence, a sense of floating, and feelings of frustration. As they did not want to report their experience to their family members or the police, they had to bear much psychological pressure on themselves.

Thus, as regards the state of body and mind of the sexually exploited and sexually abused youth and children, they were all in a highly endangered state of being infected with AIDS and STDs, and suffering from gynaecological problems as well as pregnancy. This was due to the lack of understanding or misuse of self-protection. Psychologically, all the sexually exploited and sexually abused children suffered from feelings of inferiority. This contributed to their being unable to leave commercial sex work.

54

(c) Available services/gaps in services

No organizations offer special services for sexually abused and sexually exploited children and youth. While government agencies and NGOs do offer services for children, they are not tailored for such children and youth. The majority of these services are located in the main city of Kunming.

The drug rehabilitation centre in Kunming is mainly responsible for drug rehabilitation, medical treatment and legal consultation, cultural publicity, ethics and psychological education among the detained drug addicts. Its objective is mainly to help the children and youths (drug addicts) in special rehabilitation and training. Some of the children at the centre are sexually abused and sexually exploited children and youth.

The repatriation station of Kunming City is subordinate to the city's civil administration bureau, and is responsible for collecting and repatriating those who have no identity cards as well as trafficked girls and women (including both domestic and cross-border). This station can only offer simple medical services.

The Save the Children Fund is currently the only foreign NGO specially servicing the children in Kunming. Its work focuses mainly on training and some projects related to children, such as the conduct of training for children to understand the Convention on the Rights of the Child.

Some other medical departments, such as hospitals and STD clinics, supply medical services. However, children must pay for these services.

Outside Kunming, the services are quite limited. In Quijing, there is only one institution which is responsible for re-educating young prostitutes and clients captured by the police. The centre does provide the girls with medical treatment and with limited psychological and legal services. In Jihong, the women's federation and youth league conduct legal training and law dissemination about the rights of women and children. The judicial department of Xishuangbanna also provides a consultation centre for women and children, supported by the Save the Children Fund which gives women and children legal aid and psychological support.

(d) Case studies

The following is a case in which the girl's parents were divorced.

When Dan Dan was 12 years old, her parents divorced. Both she and her younger sister were living with their mother after the divorce. Soon after that, her parents established families separately; her stepfather was cool towards her and her sister. Her mother bought a bus to carry passengers, but unfortunately she died in a traffic accident. Neither the father nor the stepfather was willing to take care of Dan Dan and her little sister. In order to make money and bring up her sister, she finally decided to follow a group of people in her own village and leave for Guangzhou, where they sent her to a hairdresser's shop. Her job was to wash hair for clients in the daytime and sell her body at night. A year later, she came back to offer a porno-graphic service or sell her body in a night club in Kunming.

The following is the case of a girl being trafficked by her boyfriend.

Xiao Lan is a girl from the north-east of China. After graduation from a senior high school, she met a boy, fell in love and had sexual relations with him. Half a year later, she was glad to hear that her boyfriend and another man wanted to take her and another girl south to Kunming for sightseeing. However, when they arrived at Kunming railway station, some men from Kunming came up to them, and asked them to stop at an inn near the station. Later, Xiao Lan and the other girl were told that they had already been sold to the Kunming men, who forced them to sell their bodies. If they did not obey, they would be whipped or suffer a good beating. The men had also injected heroin into the girls' veins. They had to be subordinated to the men's arrangements once their drug addiction functioned. The men bought the girls' clothes, cosmetics and supplied board and lodging to them. The girls stayed at a small inn and were taken to another hotel to offer sexual services when the men made a deal with clients. After the men had taken money from the clients, Xiao Lan and the other girl were asked to follow the clients to enter a room to offer sexual services. Xiao Lan tried five times to escape but failed. She suffered a good beating every time she was captured. She eventually succeeded in escaping from the men the sixth time. She ran to another city and worked as a waitress in a restaurant. However, later, her drug addiction worsened and, she had to act as a "Zuotai" girl at a night club, offering sexual services to clients. While working at the restaurant, she fell in love with a boy; she therefore only offered a pornographic service but did not sell her body when acting as a "Zuotai" girl. Later, because she was taking drugs, she was captured by the police and put into a drug rehabilitation centre. She now wants very much to give up taking drugs and establish a happy family with her boyfriend after leaving the centre. If it does not work, she feels she will lose confidence in any man and be able to do nothing but go back to her hometown and live alone for the rest of her life.

3. Lao People's Democratic Republic

Thirty-eight girls were interviewed, aged between 14 and 18 years. These girls engaged in commercial sex work in entertainment establishments or private houses. They shared similar backgrounds, physical and psychosocial conditions and level of education. They were usually children of rural, farming families, although some girls' parents were soldiers, government officers, doctors or merchants. Their families ranged in size from 2 to 15 children. Their educational levels ranged from none to third year of upper secondary school, and none of them had any useful vocational training.

(a) Causes of sexual exploitation

Researchers found that sexual exploitation mainly took place in entertainment establishments such as night clubs, local pubs, hotels, guest houses and private homes, where the girls were (i) required to sit with men and encourage them to drink beer; (ii) paid a percentage of the beer profits; (iii) encouraged by girlfriends who were engaged in commercial sex to make "easy" money by having sex with customers; (iv) paid high prices for sex (especially virgins and young girls); (v) molested by the drunken customers; (vi) sometimes well-treated by the pub owners, which motivated the sexually exploited children to remain at the pubs; and (vii) too intoxicated to make rational decisions.

Children of poor socio-economic families were most vulnerable to becoming involved in sexual exploitation because (i) survival demanded that these girls take on any form of job, even commercial sex, regardless of the dangers involved; (ii) some parents encouraged their girls to earn money through commercial sex; (iii) some children migrated to the cities to be relieved of the family problems which were common to broken families where parents were divorced or separated; (iv) some parents were not aware that their children were earning income through commercial sex; and (v) in other cases, parents knew that their children were engaged in prostitution but lacked the power or the will to stop them, usually because they were financially dependent on their children for survival.

A low educational level and lack of vocational training prevented the girls from acquiring well-paying jobs, which caused them to rely on prostitution for income. Neither proper education nor vocational training was available in the rural areas.

Furthermore, girls with a history of rape, sexual abuse or any other form of abusive relationship with men were most vulnerable to sexual exploitation because (i) their experience of pain and abuse made them feel insecure and depressed; (ii) such girls were ostracized in their society and could not find decent employment or ideal marriage partners; and (iii) such girls could easily justify their engaging in prostitution given the lack of opportunities to normalize their lives. In addition, pressure from friends to enter prostitution was common and influential, particularly for those who had been already sexually exploited.

Many girls said that working in factories, the other available employment option, was too difficult and low paid; that was why they chose to engage in prostitution instead, which they considered to be "more comfortable." Male customers demanded girls for their virginity and less risk of STDs, and thus pub owners and sex traders sought to recruit particularly young girls. Children who migrated to Thailand illegally in search of work, and glue-sniffing street children (usually boys), were vulnerable to many forms of exploitation by adults. Brokers were both males and females.

In addition, rapid urban growth enticed rural children to migrate to the cities but, without adequate vocational skills, they could not find lucrative jobs. The rural regions being underdeveloped, also failed to provide employment opportunities for the girls. In addition, the majority of people lacked awareness of children's rights; and laws related to child labour and prostitution were not effectively enforced.

Many factors prevented sexually exploited children from leaving their situation. The accumulation of debts to pub owners and/or merchants from whom the girls had purchased cosmetics, clothes and jewellery gave the entertainment establishment owners a strong influence over the girls. In addition, their need for a well-paying job as well as their becoming accustomed to viewing prostitution as an acceptable occupation contributed to hindering sexually exploited children from leaving.

(b) Factors affecting physical health

The research found that the interviewed girls who were engaged in commercial sex were practising behaviour which put them at risk of contracting STDs, becoming pregnant and suffering from long-term health problems. The behaviour included misuse or lack of use of birth control and condoms, excessive drinking of alcohol and smoking. The interviewees looked thin, pale, weak and sleepy. Their poor physical condition could have been a result of long working hours and lack of proper medical attention. Some of them already had major health problems.

Living conditions were expressed as being adequate and comfortable by some girls, but uncomfortable by others. Based on the fact that these girls were living in communal arrangements provided by the pub owners, it was likely that such living conditions were not of the ideal, clean type and were thus likely to have deleterious health effects.

It was found that the girls earned a modest income. Many girls sent a significant portion of their income back home and also spent heavily on purchases of beer, cigarettes, clothes and jewellery.

According to almost all of the girls interviewed, the customers usually controlled the use of condoms. Many girls did use condoms for protection. However, the girls who did not use them were at high risk of contracting STDs, a common one being gonorrhoea. Infections were often difficult to treat because the girls drank alcohol excessively, cancelling out the effects of antibiotics. They were also at high risk of contracting the AIDS virus. Furthermore, many girls lacked knowledge about the proper use of birth control. Misconceptions about birth control techniques, medicine and devices, and also termination of pregnancy using over-the-counter medicine, subjected the girls to high risk of reproductive health complications.

All the interviewed girls drank alcohol and smoked cigarettes with their customers on a regular basis. Such regular consumption of alcoholic substances and stimulants is known to cause long-term physical and mental health problems related to substance abuse.

(c) Factors affecting psychosocial health

Sexually abused and sexually exploited children experienced a wide range of psychological and behavioural problems as a result of the physical and emotional trauma from sexually exploitative situations. Abnormal behaviour included being overly promiscuous, signs of trauma, depression, excessive worry and other negative feelings.

In addition, social problems which the girls experienced included lack of positive social support, exposure to negative environmental conditions, lack of alternative options for earning money, and ostracization from families, relatives and communities. Such lack of positive, social support, which resulted in feelings of isolation and depression, further reinforced exploitation because the girls had no other place of acceptance and employment other than the entertainment establishments. This was especially true in cases where the girls had become indentured by emotional and financial debt to the pub owners.

(d) Available services/gaps in services

The girls often went to the pharmacies or clinics for basic treatment. The hospitals and clinics had not kept specific records on sexually abused and sexually exploited children because they suspected that the children had lied about their identity due to shame. It was thus difficult to monitor their health problems or provide them with effective treatment. The doctors showed genuine interest in receiving the proper training necessary for treating sexually abused and sexually exploited children with greater understanding, expertise and sensitivity.

In Champassak Province, the Lao Youth Union had conducted a survey of trafficked children, and the Lao Women's Union had begun a project on sexual exploitation. These organizations were active in disseminating information about laws, policy and health education related to sexual abuse and children's rights.

The provincial police provided the most useful information about the sexually exploited children based on their records of their names and work sites. They were interested in finding alternative solutions for the children, but recognized that the provinces lacked both medical and social welfare resources.

In addition, the central level of the Department of Social Welfare has become involved in repatriating children who were exploited in Thailand by keeping track of the situation of trafficked children. It has also made a commitment to increasing employment opportunities for children.

Thus, currently in the Lao People's Democratic Republic, there are no specific services or treatment programmes available for sexually abused children, sexually exploited children and children at risk. Interviews with medical service providers and school administrators indicated that awareness about sexual abuse and sexual exploitation must be improved.

(e) Case studies of potential victims and victims of sexual exploitation

When An was 15 years old and still a virgin, a rich businessman offered her NK50,000 to have sex with him. Now she receives NK15,000 to have sex with men. She would use a condom with the men who had sexual relations with her only if she disliked them. An became pregnant for the third time but having already undergone two abortions, she did not want to abort again, fearing death and decided to keep the baby. Her friends would not talk to her and her father and brother did not yet know that she was pregnant.

Oy and La were working at small pubs and said they had not engaged in commercial sex with customers. These pubs, however, had similar alcohol sales practices as the other pubs and the girls were required to be companions to the customers in order to encourage beer sales. La was influenced to enter prostitution by her sister Kaek, who had begun to have sex with the customers for money. Oy, however, had not engaged in prostitution but her situation seemed to put her at high risk of becoming a child prostitute. The conditions in her pub were similar to those in pubs where girls were sexually exploited. She also came from a home where her parents did not support her. Her stepfather tried to rape her and she ran away from home and went to work at a sawmill. She found that the work was too difficult, and when she saw her friends working at a pub doing light work, she followed them. She was expected to drink beer with the pub customers and received NK500 per bottle. She earned at least NK60,000 per month. She was the only girl working in the shop. She said she did not like her work but she needed to send money home to her mother.

4. Myanmar

(a) Causes of sexual exploitation

An analysis of the 19 cases from the four townships of Muse, Hpa-An, Mawlamyine and Yangon revealed that the educational level of all the children was low. Only a few girls had received secondary-level education, while most of them did not complete primary education and some were illiterate.

The educational level of the parents was also low, and they all faced financial difficulties. All the children came from poor families, and thus they were easily lured by other people who promised them jobs with an attractive income. Most of the girls had no idea of the type of jobs that would be available. As a result, the initial period of employment was always a traumatic experience; however, most of the girls adjusted to their new life later on. Only a few girls were forcibly detained. Most of the girls professed to dislike the job but did not try hard to escape, perhaps owing to monetary incentives.

Another observable factor is the family environment. Most of the girls came from broken homes or from homes where there was friction. The parents were uneducated and they did not know how to raise children properly. Poverty was the main cause of that, as the parents had to work extremely hard to survive. As a result, it was difficult for them to provide the love, care and affection which a child requires.

(b) Factors affecting physical and psychosocial health

As mentioned earlier, because the children were poorly educated, they had very little knowledge about contraceptives, condoms and HIV/ AIDS. Most of the girls' responses regarding condom use indicated that they merely complied with their clients' wishes. In addition, the study revealed that the girls used the drugs, powders or ointments prescribed without actually knowing about their effectiveness.

The majority of the children were physically healthy except for some, who complained of headaches, skin infections and respiratory infections. However, most of the children were psychologically insecure. They had difficulty controlling their anger, were indecisive, restless and quarrelsome, and some preferred to stay alone. Some children were chronic runaways, and some felt that they were trapped, humiliated and lacking in confidence.

(c) Available services/gaps in services

Apart from the institutions established by the Department of Social Welfare, special service centres which offer services for sexually abused and sexually exploited children do not exist.

The Department of Social Welfare organizes and carries out training programmes in the skills of home-making, tailoring, interior decoration and toy-making for income generation in an effort to prevent the sexual abuse and sexual exploitation of children and youth in all four townships of Muse, Hpa-An, Mawlamyine and Yangon. These courses are conducted at the community level. The main objectives of these training programmes are to enable young girls to carry out income-generation activities and to provide them with some knowledge of home management.

As a curative measure, the Department has established a vocational training centre for women and girls in Yangon which accepts girls under 18 years of age sent by a court order under the 1949 Prostitution Suppression Act, and those apprehended by the police.

(d) Case studies of sexually abused and sexually exploited children

Tam, a Buddhist-Mon girl, was the youngest of eight children in her family. She lived in a wooden and thatch house with her parents and siblings. Her mother, aged 51 years, was a vendor and the breadwinner of the family, while her father, also 51 years old, did not work. Tam had studied until Grade 2 but was forced to leave school owing to an illness in which she suffered fits and convulsions. She was cared for by her older sisters.

At the age of 15 years, Tam attended a stage show with her sisters which was held in open ground. She was accidentally separated from them and she met her father's 60-year-old friend. He led her to an abandoned house, where he raped her. The girl disclosed the rape to her sisters, who then told their parents the story. Tam's family gave her full care after the traumatic experience, including medical and social care at home, as no services existed in the area. A year following the rape, Tam's illness has worsened. She acts like a young girl and spends days on end staring into space. Tam has occasional fits and has trouble sleeping through the night. She also experiences loss of appetite.

Cesa was the firstborn in a family of six children in Bago. A Bamar-Buddhist girl, she left school after Grade 4 because of poverty. Both her parents also had primary-level education. Her father had been an alcoholic and died, leaving behind his wife and children to struggle for survival. He had worked in a battery shop and his wife had sold snacks. Cesa lived with her mother and her siblings. Her younger brother and sister worked in a teashop selling food. After leaving school, Cesa went to work as a maid and then as a construction worker. She married at the age of 16 years but the marriage ended in divorce after only one year.

Cesa became a child in prostitution at the urging of her friends who were sex workers. She was introduced to her first customer, a 30-year-old Bamar man, by a guest-house owner. This first sexual encounter took place in Pathein and lasted 15 minutes. Following that first encounter, Cesa had five or six clients a day who were students and workers, ranging in age from 18 to 30 years. She received K1,000 from each customer and paid half of that amount to the owner of the guest house. Her daily income was thus K2,500. As she took some days off each month, she sent home K8,000-K10,000 a month.

Cesa worked during the day as she feared brothel raids, which occurred most frequently at night. Those working hours enabled her to sleep for eight or nine hours every night. In order to prevent pregnancy, Cesa used contraceptives and received a Garamycin injection twice a month. The majority of her clients used condoms and thus she had never contracted an STD. She did become pregnant once, however, and although she had thought of aborting the pregnancy, it eventually ended in a miscarriage. Her family was ignorant of these events. Cesa moved from one town to another and therefore never received regular medical care. She has been lucky to date, however, as she has never had any health problems.

Although Cesa dislikes being a child in prostitution, she feels that it is the only way to end her financial difficulties. Although she wants to return home, she hopes to save money first so that she can buy a house for her family. She does not want to marry again after experiencing an unhappy marriage. Cesa is 18 years old and has been engaged in commercial sex work for two years. Her mother and her siblings do not know what kind of work she does.

5. Thailand

(a) Sexual abuse of children

(i) Causes of sexual abuse

The sample of sexually abused children in the Thailand study consisted of 30 girls and 4 boys. Their age at the onset of sexual abuse ranged from 4 to 15 years. Forty-one per cent of the children were aged 12 to 15 years; 29 per cent were 4 to 7 years old; and 20 per cent were 8 to 11 years old.

Fifty-six per cent of the children were either enrolled in primary school or had completed one to six years of education. Another 21 per cent were either studying in or had completed lower secondary school. Three children had never attended school and another three were enrolled in or had completed 10 to 12 years of schooling. The sexually abused children were all Thai citizens originating from all regions of the country. In this study, the highest percentage of sexually abused children interviewees came from the central region.

The study revealed that 77 per cent of the sexually abused children had been sexually abused by a relative and 69 per cent had been sexually abused by an acquaintance. In only two cases were the sexually abused children abused by a stranger. Uncles and stepfathers were the most frequent abusers, making up 24 and 18 per cent of the total respectively. They were followed by biological fathers and cousins, at 12 per cent each. A grandfather was the abuser in one case and a brother-in-law in another. Of the acquaintances, neighbours were the most frequent abusers, at 21 per cent, followed by friends, at 9 per cent. Other abusers included a teacher, a monk, a parent's friend, a policeman and a servant.

The study showed that most of the sexually abused children were neglected by their parents and that contributed to the children's vulnerability to sexual abuse. All of their families were plagued with problems, and several were "multiple-problem" families. Those difficulties contributed to the poor functioning of the family and the inability of the parents to care for their children.

Family breakdown owing to divorce, separation or abandonment was common to 77 per cent of the sexually abused children. Some children stayed with their fathers, but most remained with their mothers. In single-parent households, the children were not closely supervised, as the parent was busy earning money to feed the family. When the mother remarried, tension surrounded the need to care for stepchildren. Poor parent-child bonding and attachment between stepfather and child often led to sexual abuse in the mother's absence.

Fifty-nine per cent of the families were poor and although the study showed that sexual abuse occurred in all socio-economic classes, poverty did contribute to the children's vulnerability to sexual abuse. In many cases, owing to economic problems, parents worked long hours and stayed at work until late at night. They left their children in the care of an adult who did not supervise the child closely, or who was an abuser himself. Cramped living conditions where adults and children shared the same sleeping quarters also increased the risk of sexual abuse. In a few cases, when older and younger children shared a room, sexual abuse occurred. In other cases, underprivileged children were enticed by abusers with candies, clothes or scholarships.

Substance abuse by adults was common to 53 per cent of the families of sexually abused children. Alcohol and drug addiction reduced the ability of parents to attend to their children and increased the likelihood of sexual abuse by an intoxicated male guardian.

Biological factors also played a role in some children's vulnerability to sexual abuse. A few children had a developmental disability and were unable to defend themselves against the abuser. In cases of severe developmental disability, the child was totally dependent on the abuser. In 21 per cent of cases, a family member suffered from a psychiatric illness which resulted in neglect of the child in some cases and sexual abuse of the child in others. Furthermore, in three cases, an unsafe school environment increased the children's vulnerability to sexual abuse.

The study showed that sexual abuse recurred in the majority of cases over a period of one month to three or more years. In 27 per cent of the cases, the sexual abuse lasted for more than two years; in 15 per cent of the cases it continued for more than a year; and in another 15 per cent it lasted for more than a month. In the cases of severe developmental disability, the children were unable to determine the length of the abuse, although they thought it had occurred for a long time.

The study further uncovered several factors that explained why the sexual abuse persisted for such long periods of time. In some cases, the abuser played a significant role in the family, such as a breadwinner, and other family members were afraid that the person's arrest would lead to a loss of income for the family. In other cases, the abuser was a powerful figure in the family or the community, such as school principal, monk or policeman, and no one dared to intervene in the abuse.

As most abusers were family members, they had easy access to the child. In cases where the child had a poor relationship with the parents, access to the child by acquaintances was facilitated.

Another important factor contributing to the perpetuation of sexual abuse of children and youth is that they often had difficulty in disclosing the crime. In this study, 60 per cent of the sexually abused children asked for help. The children confided in parents in eight cases and relatives in another six cases. Sexually abused children also sought assistance from schoolteachers in four cases, friends in three cases and a nun in one case. All of these people played a significant role in assisting the children by reporting the crime to the police or to a child protection service.

Forty-one per cent of the children, however, did not ask for help of their own accord. Relatives came to the assistance of the sexually abused children in five cases, teachers in four cases, doctors in four cases and a police officer in one case.

Children did not disclose the sexual abuse for several reasons. In some cases, they had been threatened by the abuser and the children feared that the abuser would kill them and anyone else they told. In other cases, the children were afraid that no one would believe them, particularly their mother in the case of rape by the stepfather. In cases where the child exposed the crime but was not cared for, it was more difficult for the child to disclose the sexual abuse a second time.

Following sexual abuse, the sexually abused children was victimized once again, as in most cases as it was the child who had to leave the family or the community, and not the abuser himself. After disclosure of sexual abuse, 21 children interviewed in the study had been forced to leave their homes and to go and live in a government or NGO facility. The abuser lived in or near the home and thus it was deemed unsafe for the child to stay there. Often no legal action was taken against an abuser, especially if he was a powerful community figure.

Loss of virginity before marriage, even as a result of rape, was a source of shame among Thai girls and thus sexually abused children often changed schools or moved away from their homes for fear that others would uncover the story of abuse. If the girl was pregnant as a result of the rape, she often moved away to protect the reputation of the child and the family. Once she had delivered the baby, she might have been able to return to her home.

In some cases, the child was taken out of the family by a social worker after an assessment that the family relationships were damaging to the child and there was a possibility that repeated abuse, neglect, violence or running away from home might occur. Among the children who lived in government and NGO facilities, all were satisfied with their living conditions, even though some centres were crowded and not sufficiently clean.

Some children who lived at the Homes did not want to go back to them owing to the presence of the abuser. Most children, however, longed to return home to be reunited with their families, even without guaranteed safety.

Sixty-five per cent of the families of the sexually abused children accepted the problems resulting from sexual abuse and tried to support the children. When the child moved to a Home, family members kept in contact with the child by visits, telephone calls or letters. Many parents felt guilty that they had allowed the tragedy to happen to their children. In 35 per cent of the cases, the families reacted negatively towards the sexually abused children and blamed them in order to protect the abusers, who included family members, powerful persons or parents' friends.

Most sexually abused children no longer had contact with their friends and classmates once they moved away from their school. In the Homes, the children had similar problems and thus peer rejection due to stigmatization was not a problem.

Sixty-eight per cent of the sexually abused children interviewed expected to have a better future. They hoped to further their education and find good jobs. Some children who had not yet recovered from the abuse were depressed and refused to talk about the future. Most of them wished to receive educational and career support and some also wanted help with lodging.

(ii) Factors affecting physical health

The health problems and needs of the sexually abused children interviewed for the study can be broken down into five categories: general health problems; health problems related to sexual abuse; developmental and intelligence problems; mental health problems; and risk behaviour.

a. General health problems

Most of the sexually abused children were examined by doctors, nurses and social workers. Seventy-four per cent of them were found to be in good health with no severe illnesses except for occasional colds. Nine children were found to have some illnesses, such as a peptic ulcer, motion sickness and frequent headaches.

Symptoms and signs of illness found in decreasing frequency were as follows: common cold, 21 per cent; headache and stomach-ache, 18 per cent each; skin problems and lice, 15 per cent each; malnutrition, 12 per cent; fever, dizziness and bed-wetting, 9 per cent each; nail-biting and obesity, 6 per cent each; and hypermenorrhoea, hair fallout, epilepsy and seizure from tension, 3 per cent each. Although most children did not have any serious illnesses, they had poor hygiene and they were small for their age as a result of neglect and prolonged malnutrition.

When the sexually abused children lived at home, their families cared for them when they fell ill. In 26 cases, the children were taken to a government hospital or private clinic, which provided good services. Some children did not visit medical facilities owing to the lack of a caretaker at home, poverty or residence in a remote area.

b. Health problems related to sexual abuse

The health problems cause by sexual abuse among the sexually abused children interviewed included pregnancy in five cases; gonorrhoea in four cases; tearing of genitals of young children in two cases; criminal abortion in six cases; and abortion due to pregnancy complications in one case. No screening for HIV was done among those sexually abused children interviewed, as the test was not ordered by the physician.

c. Developmental and intelligence problems

Most doctors, social workers and caseworkers noticed that many sexually abused children had developmental disabilities and were not as clever as other children. The interviews showed that many children appeared to have limited intellectual capacity.

Intellectual assessments were conducted among 16 female sexually abused children who were referred by the Centre for the Protection of Child Rights to King Chulalongkorn Memorial Hospital for the treatment of problems related to sexual abuse (including 11 sexually abused children from this study) in the period April to June 1998. Thirteen girls were found to have moderate to severe developmental disability (low average IQ of 80 to 90, three sexually abused children; borderline IQ of 70 to 80, six sexually abused children; mild mental retardation with an IQ of 50 to 70, two sexually abused children; and moderate mental retardation, with an IQ of 30 to 50, two sexually abused children).

d. Mental health problems

Alongside the traumatic experience of sexual abuse, most of the sexually abused children experienced additional stressful changes in their lives, including moving away from home, changing schools, adjusting to living in a Home, and living with the knowledge that the abuser was still at large.

The sexually abused children interviewed required a considerable amount of support to enable them to adjust to the new changes imposed on them. Many of the children, failing to cope, developed emotional and behavioural problems. All but one[5] needed continuous rehabilitation in order to help them cope effectively and not become abusers themselves in the future.

The psychological reactions of the children as a result of the abuse corresponded to the length of time which had passed since the abuse occurred. Interviews which were conducted close to the time of the abuse showed children with severe psychological reactions, such as fear, anxiety and depression. In interviews with the children that occurred several months after the sexual abuse, the children exhibited angry, aggressive and inappropriate behaviour.

The sexually abused children in this research exhibited more emotional than behavioural problems. The most common emotional problem was that of guilt, followed by fear, anxiety, irritability, hopelessness, daydreaming, post-trauma syndrome (hyper-arousal, avoidance and re-experiencing the abuse), depression, tearfulness and loneliness. The most common behavioural problem was aggressive behaviour, followed by seductive behaviour, self-hurt and attempted suicide, including jumping from a building, igniting the bedroom, sleeping pill overdose and toxic substance ingestion.

(e) Risk behaviour

Risk behaviour is an important aspect of health prevention and promotion in adolescents. Risk behaviour in this case is defined as high risk to morbidity and mortality, including accident-related behaviour, violent behaviour, suicidal behaviour, fighting, use of weapons, drug abuse and inappropriate sexual activity both to oneself and to others.

The sexually abused children in this study exhibited much risky behaviour. Self-destructive behaviour and attempted suicide by wrist-slashing and self-cutting were not uncommon. Running away from home or from the rehabilitation centre, aggressiveness, seductive

---

[5] The one girl who did not receive rehabilitation was 15 years old, and was sexually abused on one occasion by her sister's husband. There was no sexual intercourse and she received a great deal of support from her parents. In the beginning she had some psychological reactions of fear and anxiety, but later she was able to cope well. One month after the incident, she was planning to press charges against her uncle, even though his family threatened both herself and her mother.

behaviour and inappropriate sexual conduct are some examples of the problems that the staff of Homes encounter on a daily basis.

Substance abuse is also a serious risk behaviour, which was exhibited by three of the sexually abused children interviewed. One child used amphetamines and the other two children sniffed glue.

(b) Sexual exploitation of children

(i) Causes of sexual exploitation

The sexually exploited children interviewed for this study consisted of 19 girls and 10 boys, ranging in age from 7 to 17 years. The onset of sexual exploitation among the children occurred from the ages of 4 to 18 years. On average, the boys became children in prostitution at a younger age than the girls, with the youngest boy at 4 years old and the youngest girl at 11 years old. Most of the boys were children in prostitution between the ages of 6 and 10 years and the majority of girls became sexually exploited children between 11 and 15 years of age.

Seventy-six per cent of the sexually exploited children were enrolled in or had been educated at the primary level. One boy had never attended school and six girls were enrolled in or had studied in secondary school. All of the sexually exploited children were Thai citizens. Most of the girls were born in north-eastern and northern Thailand, with four girls from the central region. The boys came from eastern and central Thailand, with one boy from the north-eastern region. None of the sexually exploited children interviewed came from southern Thailand.

The sexually exploited children came from small families with parents who worked in the service, agriculture and business sectors. Sixty-five per cent of the families had one to two children and another 31 per cent came from families of three to seven children. Most of the children interviewed were either the only child or the youngest child of the family.

All of the families of the sexually exploited children, with the exception of three, experienced one or more psychosocial stressors, which increased their children's vulnerability to sexual exploitation. Family breakdown, including divorce, separation or death, was the most prevalent stressor, which was found among 80 per cent of the children interviewed. This rupture resulted in neglect of children, who then ran away from home, feeling unsupported and unloved.

Substance abuse by parents and guardians was another stressor that led to neglect of children and increased vulnerability to sexual exploitation. Alcoholism and drug abuse were common to 38 per cent of the families of sexually exploited children.

A third stressor was sexual abuse by a family member, which occurred among 31 per cent of the sexually exploited children interviewed, including seven girls and two boys.[6] When some of these children tried to escape from the abusers by running away from home, they were then re-abused or sexually exploited by other men.

Many of the girls upheld traditional attitudes regarding the sanctity of virginity before marriage. Sexual violation at a young age left them traumatized and hopeless. They felt as though they were "damaged goods" and thus could no longer marry and raise a family. Prostitution thus became an option as they felt they had nothing left to lose. Many of the girls who had been sexually abused left their homes as in many cases the abusers were resident in their village. With no place to go, many joined friends who later introduced them to commercial sex work.

A fourth stressor experienced by 35 per cent of families of the sexually exploited children was poverty. Some children, particularly girls, became sexually exploited children in order to earn money to care for family members who were ill or to assist family members in servicing debts. Traditionally, daughters have a duty to care for their parents, whereas sons are expected to marry and care for their new family. Poverty, however, also pushed the male sexually exploited children in this study, particularly the street children, into commercial sex work. In most cases they worked in order to earn quick money to meet their own basic needs or to purchase drugs.

In a few cases, no psychosocial stressors existed in the families of the sexually exploited children, who saw prostitution as a good job where money could be made quickly and easily. They used the money they earned to buy material possessions, including brand-name clothing, which they had coveted since they were young, or drugs. Some of the sexually exploited children sent money home to their parents to build a new and bigger house or to buy a television set or a motorcycle.

---

[6] In addition, two other boys did not provide information regarding past sexual abuse.

Another contributing factor to children's entry into prostitution revealed in this study was their contact with acquaintances or relatives working in the commercial sex industry. Several of the sexually exploited children were convinced to enter prostitution by commercial sex workers dressed in expensive clothing and jewellery who boasted of their large earnings.

Some of the girls had had sexual relations voluntarily with their boyfriends as they did not believe that maintaining one's virginity before marriage was important. They enjoyed sexual activity and worked as free-lance prostitutes, as the profession was lucrative.

All of the female sexually exploited children interviewed in the study became children in prostitution voluntarily. Seven girls had been led into prostitution by friends, five by neighbours, three by relatives, including a mother, and four went into it on their own. In the case of the boys, four had become children in prostitution of their own accord, three had been led by a friend, one had followed a relative, one had been kidnapped and another deceived.

The sexually exploited children had worked as children in prostitution for periods ranging from three weeks to five years. Seventy-two per cent of the children had worked in the commercial sex industry for more than one year.

While working as children in prostitution, the lifestyles of the sexually exploited children differed depending on the type of commercial sex work in which they engaged. Three girls worked in restaurants that were also brothels and each of them rented a small room from the owner for B20 per day. Although the rooms were clean and in good condition, the ventilation was poor. After saving some money, some girls rented a larger room further away from the restaurant.

Street children who worked as prostitutes were malnourished and lived in poor and unhygienic conditions. Without any permanent shelter, the children slept on the street and wandered between neighbourhoods and sometimes from one province to another. These children had no money to buy food or clothing and sold sexual services in order to stay alive and to buy drugs, especially glue. The compensation that this group received was very small compared with that of other types of prostitutes.

73

At the time of the interviews, all of the children were participating in the rehabilitation programmes of the government and private sectors, with the exception of four girls, who were still working as prostitutes in restaurants. The children were brought to the Homes by police, caseworkers of private organizations, and in one case by an acquaintance. Four girls came of their own accord.

Forty-five per cent of the families of the sexually exploited children accepted their child's profession, as several children sent money home. Other parents were happy to be relieved of the financial responsibility of caring for their child. Another 45 per cent of the families did not accept that their children worked in prostitution. This rejection, however, originated from poor parent-child relationships, which began long before the children began to work as prostitutes. Three children had no contact whatsoever with their families. One was an orphan, another had been kidnapped and the third had run away from home.

Most of the female sexually exploited children expected to have a better future. Some felt ashamed that they had worked as children in prostitution while others felt that they would not be stigmatized for having worked in the sex industry. In some cases, they felt that they would have an advantage over other single women as they were wealthier and men would thus like them more. The male sexually exploited children felt that their future would improve as they were receiving help and lodging.

(ii) Factors affecting physical health

The sexually exploited children interviewed in the study had health problems and needs which can be categorized into five categories as follows: general health problems; health problems related to sexual activity; developmental and intelligence problems; mental health problems; and risk behaviour.

a. General health problems

Of the sexually exploited children interviewed in the study, 18 were found to be healthy. The remaining six girls and five boys suffered from various ailments. Street children in particular were unhealthy, undernourished and had poor hygiene. Upon physical examination, they were found to be small for their age and had skin problems, including lice, fungal infections, eczema and impetigo.

Symptoms and signs of illnesses found in decreasing frequency were as follows: headache and skin disease, 38 per cent; malnutrition, 24 per cent; chest pain, 17 per cent; stomach-ache and bed-wetting, 14 per cent; common cold, fatigue, lice and insomnia, 10 per cent; motion sickness and arthralgia, 7 per cent; and anaemia, asthma, toothache and nose pain resulting from plastic surgery, 3 per cent.

Interviews focusing on the care the children received while staying at home revealed good care during illness. Most families (21 cases) took their children to government hospitals or private clinics. There was no problem regarding access to health care, medical facilities and the quality of services they received. Three children had problems paying for the medical expenses due to poverty. For four children, the hospital was very far from home. One child could not remember how he was taken care of during the illness.

b. Health problems related to sexual activity

Eleven sexually exploited children, including nine girls and two boys, had contracted a STD. The most common forms were gonorrhoea and non-specific urethritis. One five-year-old street child had chronic syphilitic infection of the anus. Of the sexually exploited children, four girls and one boy were seropositive for the AIDS virus. Of these five, two had full-blown AIDS at the time of the interview, with symptoms of malaise, recurrent fever, arthritis, skin disease and lung infection. Only four of the children knew their HIV status, while the fifth, a boy, had not been told the result of his blood test.

One girl became pregnant with her boyfriend. The staff at the rehabilitation centre where she lived cared for her well and she received good support from her peers. However, owing to the tight budget of the centre, the meals provided were not nutritious enough for a pregnant woman.

Girls who worked as direct and indirect prostitutes did not have difficulty in obtaining health care because most sex establishments are concerned about "cleanliness". As part of the VD control programme of the Ministry of Public Health, these sex establishments are registered and VD clinic officers visit them periodically. The owner of the sex establishment also sends the prostitutes to the VD clinic for a physical check-up every week and for HIV and syphilis blood tests every three months.

Although prostitutes below the age of 18 years are concealed, the girls interviewed in the study all received regular check-ups by various means. Some lied about their age and others used the identification card of a friend who was over 18 years old. In many cases, the sexually exploited children reported their true age to the VD clinic staff when they realized that they were not police and thus could not arrest them. The staff emphasized that telling them the truth about their age would enable them to take better care of the child's health.

Children in prostitution at highest risk of STDs, including HIV infection, were those working as free-lance and street prostitutes. In the former group, no regular check-ups were imposed on the children and they felt immune from STDs. Some young schoolgirls sold sex for fun and never used any method of protection, such as a condom, seriously and consistently. Their negotiating power with adult customers was also limited.

Street children had inadequate health care for reasons such as poverty, lack of adult supervision and frequent moves. Other reasons for not seeking medical treatment included fear of being sent into the care of the Department of Public Welfare by the hospital and thereby relinquishing their freedom.

c. Developmental and intelligence problems

Four of the sexually exploited children, including two girls and two boys, showed limited intellectual capacity. A complete assessment of one boy showed moderate developmental disability with an IQ of 69.

d. Mental health problems

Interviews with the sexually exploited children revealed that the three most common emotional problems were sadness (55.2 per cent), hopelessness (55.2 per cent), and irritability (41.4 per cent). Other problems experienced included tearfulness, worthlessness, anxiety, lack of motivation, daydreaming and loneliness. The three most prevalent behavioural problems were lying (34.5 per cent), withdrawal (31 per cent), and suicidal feelings (31 per cent). Further problems included self-hurt, quarrelsomeness, stealing, destruction of property and aggressiveness.

e. Risk behaviour

The sexually exploited children were at high risk of several health problems owing to their risky behaviour. In addition to unsafe sexual practice, they exhibited violent behaviour towards both themselves and others.

Drug abuse was another type of risk behaviour in which several sexually exploited children engaged. In this study, 12 girls and 3 boys used drugs, including amphetamines, in nine cases, cigarettes in five cases, alcohol in two cases and glue in one case. More female sexually exploited children were found to use drugs in this study as they were older and some of them still worked as children in prostitution. Others were in rehabilitation programmes that were not strict. The boys were younger and participated in strict government programmes.

(c) Caregivers

(i) Medical caregivers

Twenty-three physicians who work with sexually abused and sexually exploited children were interviewed for this study, including paediatricians, gynaecologists, psychiatrists and general practitioners from Bangkok and other provinces.

a. Profile of children in care

Most of the cases that were referred to the physicians were sexually abused children cases. The number of sexually abused children that each physician cared for ranged from 2 to 50, depending on the doctor's speciality and years of service. In general, paediatricians and child psychiatrists treated more cases of sexually abused children than general practitioners. Physicians in larger hospitals, especially those affiliated with a university or those that act as referral centres, treat the largest number of cases of sexually abused children.

Most of the physician's sexual abused cases were girls. The abusers were family members or acquaintances of the child, including teachers, monks and officers of organizations working with children. Physicians in the north had referrals of girls from ethnic minorities and from Myanmar. The physician in the south, where the Islam religion prevails, reported very few cases of sexual abuse of children.

b. Health issues

Most of the sexually abused children were in good health. Common problems which they experienced were those which resulted from sexual abuse, including STDs and pregnancy. In some cases, complications related to pregnancy arose owing to the young age of the mother and thus the foetus was aborted in order to save the mother's life. In addition, some of the children took drugs such as amphetamines.

The physicians estimated that half of the sexually abused children they treated suffered from intellectual disabilities ranging from slight to severe. The psychological problems encountered among sexually exploited children varied depending on the child's age, as well as the nature and duration of the sexual abuse. Some children were depressed and fearful. One paediatrician reported the case of a child who was sold to an agent and later developed psychosis.

All of the physicians interviewed agreed that sufficient medical services existed to treat sexually abused children and no special services needed to be developed to deal with such cases. The existing services, however, needed to be organized to increase efficiency. Clear and concise guidelines were needed on how to handle cases of sexually abused children as well as on when and where to refer the cases.

c. Problems encountered in caring for sexually abused children

The physicians interviewed encountered several common problems in caring for sexually abused children, which are described below.

- Families do not always cooperate in providing information and bringing the children back to the hospital for follow-up visits. They often fear disclosure. As many of the abusers are family members, the families fear the arrest of the abuser should they take the child back to the hospital for a second visit. This results in inadequate treatment of the child.

- Physicians must on many occasions testify in court. However, as confidentiality is important for the therapy process, physicians often find it difficult to maintain the trust of the sexually abused children following testimony.

- Health professionals are not guaranteed safety, and treating cases of sexually abused children may put them in danger, especially when the abusers are antisocial or when they have power in the community.

- Comprehensive health care is almost impossible in cases when the sexually abused child is sent to another area to live because no organization exists to help to coordinate care. In most provinces, no organizations exist to assist sexually abused children apart from the Department of Public Welfare. Its work has many limitations, including several rules and restrictions which reduce the speed and flexibility of its work. Thus, many children from all regions of the country are often referred to NGOs based in Bangkok.

- The interrogation process and court procedures have a negative impact on the child's mental health, and affect the physician's care for the child. Treatment usually focuses on the individual child without including the family and thus is not sufficiently holistic.

- Sexually abused children are often not brought in immediately after they experience sexual abuse and thus their health needs are often complex. In one case, a child had developed a severe pelvic infection resulting from gonorrhoea and had to undergo a major operation.

- Most hospitals do not have specific and clear guidelines on procedures for treating. Further, no effective cooperation or networking exists between hospitals. Long-term follow-up on cases of sexually abused children is rare as there are too few social workers. Some 300- to 400-bed hospitals only have two social workers. The large caseload makes it impossible for them to follow up the cases of sexually abused children which constitute a small percentage of the total caseload.

(ii) Psychosocial caregivers

Twenty-three caseworkers, including 4 men and 19 women, were interviewed. Their ages ranged from 23 to 50 years. Four of them work in the government sector and 19 in three private organizations. The duration of work ranged from one month to 20 years, with an average of two to five years. Seventeen caseworkers have received some training in caring for sexually abused children.

a. Profile of children in care

The psychosocial caregivers interviewed stated that care for sexually abused and sexually exploited children comprised only a small proportion of their caseload. Although most of the cases were Thai girls, on occasion they also treated children from ethnic minorities as well as those from Yunnan Province (China), the Lao People's Democratic Republic and Myanmar.

The problems that the psychosocial caregivers encountered in their care for sexually abused and sexually exploited children included both personal and case management problems.

b. Factors affecting physical health

Most of the sexually abused and sexually exploited children with whom the caregivers came into contact were in good health and

therefore in most cases no special medical care was needed. Their
health problems consisted of the common cold and gastritis.

Those children who lived on the street or in a slum were
neglected and often came from ethnic minorities. Most of them were
small for their age, with poor hygiene and poor health. They usually
had skin disease such as tinea, lice and pyoderma.

Although the staff persons have taught the children about
hygiene and skin care, the problems still recur because some centres
are crowded and insufficiently clean. Aside from skin problems, many
children also have dental problems such as cavities. As teeth are a
hidden part of the body, related problems do not receive sufficient
attention.

Five to ten per cent of sexually abused and sexually exploited
children whom the caregivers treated were seropositive for the AIDS
virus. There were almost no cases of HIV/AIDS infection among the
sexually abused children, while the prevalence in the sexually exploited
children was as high as 50 per cent in some provinces in northern
Thailand.

The caregivers experienced difficulties in caring for the children
living with HIV/AIDS as they had difficulties in adjusting to the
Home and were often depressed. In some cases, their family members
never visited them and others were disowned by their families because
of the negative stigma attached to the disease.

Another problem which arose with caregivers in relation to
children who were seropositive for the AIDS virus was confidentiality
and disclosure to the child. In some centres, the blood test results are
not revealed to the children for fear that the infected child would be
rejected. Other centres, however, disclose the results and teach
children to care for themselves as well as to protect themselves from
infection.

In several centres, fearing negative consequences, staff members
have not been able to decide whether or not to disclose the results of
the blood tests, and to whom the information should be revealed.

The interviews with the caregivers showed that drug abuse was
more prevalent in sexually exploited children than in sexually abused
children. Most sexually exploited children who work in sex establishments smoke cigarettes, drink alcohol, and take amphetamines and
sleeping pills. Some of the sexually exploited children also use
stimulants to increase their sexual arousal.

Street children predominantly smoke marijuana and cigarettes, and take amphetamines. In some centres, drug use among children is difficult to control. The substance abusers also persuade other children to follow them.

c. Factors affecting psychosocial health

The most common psychological problems found by caregivers among children in rehabilitation centres were aggressive behaviour, volatile emotions and depression. Other problems include inappropriate behaviour, unwillingness to follow rules, difficulty in adjusting to life in the centre, calling for attention, and anxiety regarding themselves, their family and their future.

Fighting and hurting others were further problems encountered by caregivers at the centres. Some children turned their aggression on themselves in the forms of self-cutting and wrist-slashing. Some girls slashed their wrists prior to arriving at the centre, while others did so at the centre, following the action of their peers. Attempted suicide is not a rare event and in some centres as many as 70 per cent of the children engaged in these acts of self-mutilation.

Inappropriate sexual behaviour, including preoccupation with sexual issues, exposing their own sexual organs and seductiveness, is common among sexually abused and sexually exploited children. The psychosocial caregivers found that each child had severe and complicated problems. Instead of approaching the caregivers, the children often tried to solve the problems in their own way, which resulted in self-mutilation and fighting. Many of the children did not want to leave their families and they did not see the use of staying at the centre. For this reason, they disobeyed rules and they did not work on their problems.

d. Case management problems

Caregivers identified the following problems related to families:

- Families do not cooperate with the staff members, as previously mentioned.

- Families also need help but the centres lack the necessary budget and personnel to assist them.

- Families prefer to enter into a settlement, instead of filing charges against the abuser, so that the process can finish quickly. This results in a higher probability that re-abuse will occur.

- Families live far away and thus follow-up is often difficult and rehabilitation cannot be continued once the child has returned home.

- Caregivers do not receive protection for their work and their safety is not guaranteed. During fieldwork, they can be threatened, especially in cases when the abuser or the sex establishment owner is a powerful person in the community. Care providers are predominantly female, and many of them feel vulnerable. Even when they receive a police escort to conduct their fieldwork they are not always guaranteed safety.

- The personality and the habits of the caregivers can also be obstacles to rehabilitation work. Some caregivers are not strict enough while others are too sensitive, making the management of the children and their problems difficult.

- Caregivers who lack knowledge and experience are unable to analyse cases thoroughly or plan treatment effectively. On several occasions, they conduct their work on a trial-and-error basis and the results are poor.

- Hard work and no career advancement lead several caregivers to quit their job after a short period of time. Rehabilitation work with the children and many preventive activities thus come to a halt and children feel rejected. In one case, a girl had six different caregivers attending to her in a period of six months. She exhibited several behavioural problems when the fifth one left her job.

- Caregivers experience high levels of stress and burnout as their work is difficult and the problems the children experience are not easily solved. Many sexually exploited children, after leaving the centre, return to prostitution, leaving caregivers discouraged.

- Most caregivers carry out several jobs at once owing to staff shortages, which can result in poor performance or additional problems. If a caseworker is on call, she may not be able to supervise the children in the home closely and fighting or attempted suicide can occur. A second problem which results from the shortage of staff is that fieldwork is affected and only a limited number of children outside the centre can be cared for. Children who need help are often put on a waiting list.

- Cooperation and coordination among caregivers are often lacking, as meetings are not held on a regular basis. Caregivers are often unaware of the cases treated by their colleagues. Thus, when they are on call, their ability to solve emergency problems is reduced. In addition to this, staff members approach cases using varying methodologies and thus the work of the centre does not progress in the same direction.

- Many caregivers lack knowledge and experience in therapeutic work with children, thus affecting rehabilitative work, including psychological treatment. Caregivers are often young college graduates who lack the necessary working experience to treat traumatized and disturbed children. As a result, many children leave programmes as disturbed as when they arrived.

- Rehabilitative activities are limited and they are not carried out on a regular basis. Some activities are not appropriate for children.

- In centres that are crowded, younger children stay with older ones and they imitate the inappropriate behaviour of their elders.

- Some centres have an insufficient budget and inadequate resources, such as the lack of a car, which makes work, including home visits, difficult and slow.

In networking, the following problems were experienced by caseworkers:

- Many centres do not receive good cooperation from the police.

- Some children have specific problems, such as severe hyperactivity or learning difficulties, and thus require special education, which is unavailable.

- Caregivers, including the police, attorneys, doctors and teachers, have varying policies, ideas and methods in their work. Problems therefore arise in cooperation and team work.

- There is a lack of organizations to accept referrals, particularly outside Bangkok.

- When the staff of the centres consult physicians several problems arise, such as slow service, long waiting lists, lack of child psychiatrists, infrequent scheduling of visits, lack of discussion between psychiatrists and caregivers owing to time limitations, and no regular follow-up.

- There is a lack of hospitals that are open to treating AIDS patients. Children of ethnic minority groups living with HIV/AIDS have a particularly difficult time obtaining treatment as they are often refused admission owing to their illegal immigration status.

- Counselling services are insufficient.

- Most of the caregivers interviewed were satisfied with their job, which they find fun, challenging and exciting. They feel that their work is worthwhile and are proud to be able to help children and, in doing so, the society. The longer caregivers have worked in their job, the more attached to the children they become. Those who work in NGOs like the flexible system, which allows them to work to their full potential.

- Some caseworkers are exhausted because their work is difficult. They become discouraged as there are several aspects of their work which cannot be improved or corrected. With an excessive workload and a multitude of responsibilities, caseworkers feel that they are not doing their best at anything.

- In centres where caregivers perform night duty, some lack personal time. Most of them however, are satisfied with their salaries, especially those who work for NGOs, as they receive higher pay in general than government officers. Some caregivers are unsatisfied with their earnings as they are substantially lower than those of their colleagues in the private sector in other fields of work. Unlike government workers, NGO workers have no job security and have limited advancement opportunities. They also lack the health care and insurance privileges of their government counterparts.

- All of the caregivers interviewed expressed feelings of inadequacy of knowledge as well as experience in dealing with sexually abused and sexually exploited children. The children they care for have many psychological problems and they require further training in order to conduct rehabilitative work more effectively. Although many of the caregivers have received some training in the past, they all wish to receive further training in the following areas:

  - Child psychology and child development

  - Working with adolescents

  - Interview techniques, including establishing trust with the child and the family

  - Principles of psychiatric treatment

  - Detection of abnormality in children

  - Analysis of a child's problem and provision of appropriate treatment

- Principles of rehabilitation

- Behaviour modification techniques

- Individual and family counselling

- Principles of social welfare

- Psychological tests and the use of simple tests for assessment and follow-up

(d) *Services available to sexually abused and sexually exploited children and youth*

The study showed that services for sexually abused and sexually exploited children exist in the form of prevention programmes, shelters, training opportunities, medical services and psychosocial care in Thailand. Most of these services, however, are offered by organizations that are located in Bangkok and its surrounding area.

In the north, the provinces of Chiang Rai has four main organizations, Chiang Mai three, and Phitsanulok one main organization, serving sexually abused and sexually exploited children. In the north-east, Nong Khai, Udon Thani and Nakhon Ratchasima provinces all have one organization. Chonburi and Rayong provinces in the east have two organizations and one organization respectively. Phuket, in southern Thailand, also has just one organization.

Of the 27 organizations that serve the needs of sexually abused and sexually exploited children, 13 are governmental, 12 are non-governmental, and two are joint initiatives. The strength of these organizations lies in this cooperation, which is outlined below.

(i) *Joint efforts*

When a case of child sexual exploitation or child sexual abuse is reported to the police, a government or NGO caseworker will assist them in investigating the case. Legal matters are handled by the police, an attorney and the caseworker. If the results of the investigation show that the child is unsafe in his or her residence, he or she will be taken to a safer place such as an emergency shelter, a correction home or a rehabilitation centre. There the child receives a physical and psychological assessment, which is performed by a nurse or a psychologist. Sometimes children are examined by a paediatrician and a psychiatrist at a hospital.

From the medical and psychosocial assessment, a rehabilitation plan is established for each child with the aim of reintegrating the child into the community. The steps followed in caring for sexually abused or sexually exploited children include reporting of the sexual abuse and sexual exploitation; fact-finding; the legal process; child protection; rehabilitation; and reintegration of the child into society.

Child sexual abuse and sexual exploitation cases are complex and their management requires cooperation among various disciplines. Efforts have been made by Chulalongkorn University, Chiang Mai University and Songkla Nakarin University to establish a multidisciplinary team approach in dealing with sexually abused and sexually exploited children. One team is composed of a paediatrician, a child psychiatrist, a social worker, a nurse, a forensic internist, a psychologist, and representatives of NGOs or the Department of Public Welfare. The aim of the effort is to coordinate the services delivered by various organizations in order to provide sexually abused and sexually exploited children with comprehensive care.

The services available to sexually abused and sexually exploited children in Thailand can be divided into three major categories, including medical care, psychosocial care, and legal assistance.

(ii) Medical care for sexually abused children

When family members of sexually abused children seek assistance, they often go to health professionals for treatment of their children's physical or emotional problems. Public awareness has been heightened in recent years about child sexual abuse through government-sponsored campaigns and thus evaluation and advice are now sought more frequently from psychiatrists than in the past.

At the hospital, the sexually abused child is examined by either the paediatrician, in order to assess physical injury, or by the child psychiatrist, in the absence of physical injury. The child may then be referred to other health professionals as needed. A social worker will manage the case, which includes coordinating the treatment provided, working with the family and following up on the case.

In the past few years, efforts have been made to improve the services provided to maltreated children, especially sexually abused children. Professionals now realize that their past bureaucratic procedures had often caused the sexually abused children or sexually exploited children to suffer further. Efforts have been made to improve the system in this regard, including greater coordination of interviews among doctors so that the child is not asked the same question by more than one doctor and not putting such children on a waiting list in view of the seriousness of the matter.

At Chiang Mai University, the Centre for the Prevention and Protection of Children's Rights has been established, with the cooperation of the Governor, the government and private sectors, Maharaj Hospital and the Faculty of Medicine of Chiang Mai University. Guidelines were established to reorganize services into a "one-stop service" and to coordinate the work of the Suspected Child Abuse and Neglect Team.

When a sexually abused child enters the hospital, the outpatient card will be stamped "secret" in order to maintain confidentiality. No information will be recorded on the card and all of the relevant information regarding the sexual abuse and the medical condition of the child will be recorded in a special report, which is kept in an envelope stamped "secret". This envelope is kept in the office of the social worker in the Outpatients' Department.

If the child has been physically injured, he or she will receive first-aid treatment. The child will then be interviewed by a social worker, who then contacts other departments and health professionals in the Suspected Child Abuse and Neglect Team as appropriate. If the child needs a physical or gynaecological examination, a specialist and not an intern will conduct it.

(iii) Medical care for sexually exploited children

Medical care for sexually exploited children differs from that for sexually abused children. Only those who work in sex establishments that are registered with the Division for Venereal Disease Control of the Ministry of Public Health receive regular medical care. Sex establishment owners send sexually exploited children to the VD clinics for a physical check-up (pelvic examination) weekly, and blood tests are conducted for syphilis and HIV every three months. If an establishment owner does not send sexually exploited children for regular check-ups, the VD clinic officer will visit the establishment to try to persuade the owner and the girls to seek health care.

When a sexually exploited child is infected with an STD, she is interviewed about the place and time of contraction. The VD officer will then visit the establishment in which she works to convince the owner of the importance of health check-ups for the other sexually exploited children. Most owners cooperate, as they are concerned about the standard of the services they offer. If their clients contract a disease, they will stop frequenting the establishment.

Sexually exploited children who test positive for HIV are counselled and then sent home by the brothel owner. Many sexually exploited children, however, move to another province and continue the same work, thus making it difficult to control the spread of AIDS in the country.

Apart from venereal diseases and other STDs, such as fungal infection and trichomonal infection, some commercial sex workers experience problems related to abortion. A VD clinic officer reported that more than 50 per cent of the prostitutes who visited his clinic had aborted once or twice.

Another frequent problem of children in prostitution is the use of condoms. Children in prostitution cannot negotiate with their customers in the same way as adult prostitutes can. The rate of condom use among children in prostitution is therefore lower than in adult prostitutes and the health of the sexually exploited children is affected. A second problem is that when children in prostitution contract a STD, it is difficult for them to obtain treatment from government hospitals because child prostitution is illegal and they may be arrested and sent to a correction home.

The Division for VD Control also conducts preventive health programmes for prostitutes. The officers visit sex establishments, and observe the workplace and the living conditions of sex workers. They will discuss the benefits of regular medical check-ups with owners and sex workers, and try to persuade them to visit a clinic. Meetings are sometimes arranged with the sex workers in order to educate them about hygiene, STDs, AIDS, protection methods and prevention of diseases. Topics such as stress management and making choices for a happy life are also included in the meetings, to help to raise the standard of living of commercial sex workers.

(iv) Psychosocial care for sexually abused and sexually exploited children

Psychosocial care for sexually abused and sexually exploited children is provided by both the public and private sectors. The government service providers are the Occupational Assistance Division and the Child Welfare Protection Division of the Department of Public Welfare, Ministry of Labour and Social Welfare. In the private sector, several organizations offer preventive services to children at high risk of sexual exploitation in order to prevent them from becoming commercial sex workers. Some organizations provide both preventive and rehabilitative services to sexually abused children as well as sexually exploited children.

a. Department of Public Welfare: rehabilitative services

The Department of Public Welfare serves sexually abused and sexually exploited children through the Occupational Assistance Division and the Child Welfare Protection Division. The former deals with child and adult prostitutes in both the preventive and rehabilitative aspects. The latter deals with other types of child maltreatment, such as sexual abuse and child labour.

There are four rehabilitation centres for children in prostitution in Thailand: Song Kwai Home in Phitsanulok Province, for sexually exploited children in northern Thailand; Nariswad Home in Nakhon Ratchasima Province, for sexually exploited children in north-eastern Thailand; Kredtrakarn Home in Nonthaburi, for sexually exploited children in central and southern Thailand; and Huaypong Home, a home for boys from throughout the country, in Rayong Province.

Children engaged in prostitution and arrested by the police for violating the Prevention and Suppression of Prostitution Act, BE 2539 (1996) are sent to these homes. When they arrive, they are interviewed and assessed by a social worker and/or a psychologist. Rehabilitation plans are made on an individual basis. Each child will remain at the rehabilitation centre for no longer than two years.

The rehabilitative programmes of these centres have five main components. The first is counselling, which includes individual counselling, group counselling and group activities to raise the self-confidence and self-esteem of the sexually exploited children. Education is a second element including a weekly tele-education class for children who have not yet completed secondary school. A third component is job training, which consists of several six-month vocational courses, such as hair-cutting, nutrition, home-making, decoration and ornament making, dress-making, cloth-weaving and beautician. Family work, including family counselling, family camp and home visits is the fourth component and medical care constitutes the last element.

The children are assessed regularly by the staff and are discharged to their homes once they are behaviourally and emotionally stable and once the family is ready to receive the child.

b. Department of Public Welfare: preventive services

The preventive services of the Department of Public Welfare centre on sexually exploited children and not sexually abused children. Various programmes exist to prevent high-risk children from entering prostitution, which include the following:

- Family Counselling Service to counsel families which experience psychosocial stress, poor relationships or inability to manage their children, in order to prevent child abuse or running away;

- Child Protection Service, to accept sexually abused and sexually exploited children back into their homes without further sexual abuse or sexual exploitation;

- Child Protection Officers, who work closely with the police and school inspectors to investigate entertainment and public places to find out if there are children with inappropriate behaviour;

- Counselling and job training to prevent the sexual abuse and sexual exploitation among vulnerable children; and

- New Life Project for Rural Women, to prevent young, undereducated girls from entering into prostitution and to prevent migration to big cities. The project provides job training and job placement service and also provides small funding to start small businesses.

Although the Department of Public Welfare has a local office in every province of Thailand which assists children who have been arrested or those who are referred to the hospital, the number of cases of sexually abused and sexually exploited children that the Department officers assist is low in comparison with NGOs. The Department engages in primarily office-based work and there is little knowledge of its work among the general public. In some provinces, only one or two cases of sexually abused children are assisted yearly, and in big cities, the number does not exceed 10 annually.

The Department offices in most provinces do not have the space to accommodate sexually abused and sexually exploited children, nor do they have caregivers on the staff to assist them. (There are only nine public welfare homes in the country.) Care for the children therefore depends on government cooperation with NGOs. Since most of these are based in Bangkok, most of the children are referred to the capital. This increases the expense of care as well as causing difficulties in adjustment for the children, who have to live far away from home.

(v) Legal services

The legal process for a sexually exploited child begins once a case has been reported or when a child has been arrested. After the child has been questioned by the police, the case is taken up by the court. The child, in the meantime, is sent temporarily to a rehabilitation centre as the police may not hold a child for more than 48 hours. If the judge decides that the child's parents cannot care for the child or that the child needs rehabilitation, he or she will be sent to a government or NGO rehabilitation centre. Under the Prevention and Suppression of Prostitution Act, BE 2539 (1996), sexually exploited children are no longer penalized, but are protected and rehabilitated.

In most sexual abuse cases, the victim and the abuser will agree on an out-of-court settlement whereby the abuser compensates the victim financially. When a settlement cannot be agreed upon, the victim's family reports the case to the police, who then play a significant role in its resolution.

Caregivers for sexually abused and sexually exploited children have raised concerns that the legal system re-abuses them by posing inappropriate questions during investigations. The child must often identify the abuser in a face-to-face setting, which makes the victim feel threatened, ashamed and guilty. Many children are left more regressed and emotionally disturbed following the investigation and identification process.

Efforts have been made in the past year to correct these problems. In the future, the government will pass a new act which will stipulate that the investigation of a child abuse case must be conducted by a child psychiatrist, a psychologist or a social worker, trained in handling cases of sexual abuse. When no such person can be located, a teacher or someone whom the child trusts could act as a substitute.

The interrogation session would be videotaped and shown in court to save the child from undergoing a second questioning. The identification of the abuser will be conducted through a one-way mirror so that the child does not have to confront the abuser. A training course in child psychology and interview techniques has been developed for police and legal officers who handle cases of sexually abused children. A videotape session of the psychiatric assessment of a child victim, conducted by a child psychiatrist at King Chulalongkorn Memorial Hospital, will be used in court for the first time in mid-1999, marking the start of a new era in care provision for sexually abused children.

6. Viet Nam

The researchers interviewed a total of 35 sexually abused children, 21 sexually exploited children and 19 children who had experienced both sexual abuse and sexual exploitation. The children ranged in age from 4 to over 24 years. Fifty-three per cent of such girls interviewed were not yet 16 years old (29 out of 54). For the two children who were younger than six years, the researchers interviewed their parents to understand the abusive situation. There were 15 girls aged 12 years and younger who were interviewed (28 per cent).

(a) Causes of sexual abuse and sexual exploitation

The children came from relatively low educational backgrounds with educational levels completed by the interviewed children ranging from having no education to having completed high school. Of the interviewed children who had experienced sexual abuse, 50 had been raped by neighbours, employers, friends or strangers. The proportion was almost the same in the towns as in the countryside. There were four cases of incest, each involving a child under six years old.

The majority of the interviewed children (76 per cent) who were involved in prostitution were born to families of either poor peasants or workers. Thirty-four of the 39 children belonged to poor house-holds in the locality where they lived and worked. Parents normally had a low level of education. Seventy to 80 per cent of the fathers and mothers had only a primary-school education and there was not much family education at home. Eighteen of the 39 children had only one parent at home (the father or mother had died or the parents were divorced). In those cases, the loss of a parent was one of the first causes of a child leaving home, as the pain or anger of the loss was too great to bear.

Sexual abuse offenders were mainly young people aged between 16 and 35 years (70 per cent). In one case, a youth offender had been exposed to a pornographic film and, not having much knowledge about sex, was curious and raped a girl as young as two to three years old. Some of the violators were older. Among the 54 cases of children enduring sexual abuse, six of the abusers were over 60 years old. In one case a man was sentenced to life imprisonment owing to his having violated his own daughter, his son's daughter and his daughter's daughter.

Several of the interviewed children were violated in their younger years, leaving them with feelings of hopelessness, shame and loneliness. These emotions, along with the pressure of assisting one's family and/or being able to live independently, and their inexperience and lack of education, led them to be lured into prostitution easily by promises of money and freedom from their oppressive situation. None of the children felt comfortable about the sexual activity in which they were involved.

In general, the sexually exploited children interviewed came from large families and were themselves the firstborn or secondborn with some responsibility for the family economy (two children were the main providers in their family). With the stress of contributing to the family welfare and no other available jobs, these children most often felt that there was no better option than to engage in commercial sex. Many of them did not want their families to know of their sexual exploitation, and thus kept it secret from their parents.

The families of some children, however, were well aware of their situation. These girls were normally illiterate or had little education and felt very little or almost no anger when their families sold them to brothels. Many of the children interviewed had left school because of the costs incurred that the family could not afford, and they needed to help with the family income. Very few sexually exploited children thought that they would be able to return to school. Having endured so much emotional damage and aware of their bad reputation, sexually exploited children avoided the embarrassment of rejoining their old friends in school.

Of the 39 interviewed children who were sexually exploited, 19 had endured sexual abuse beforehand. Six of them were children in prostitution with their own consent. Some children at age 6 to 12 years old had been raped or sold to brothels to serve the commercial needs of unscrupulous brothel masters. Some children, after having experienced the first sexual violation, were shunned by their families and did not receive any sympathy or support. Thirty-four of the 39 children had engaged in commercial sex with a person of a different sex at some point between the ages of 13 and 17 years old. A number had engaged in commercial sexual relations with persons of the same sex, especially with homosexual foreigners.

Four children came from families of the middle economic level. Each of them had become children in prostitution owing to family problems or for material reasons. However, despite the various reasons, these children found prostitution to be a good source of income, and enabled them to afford a lifestyle they enjoyed.

Thirteen of the interviewed sexually exploited children were forced to act as children in prostitution to pay debts to brothel masters or were sold as wives. Most of the children engaged in commercial sex had to stand along the road or entertain visitors in brothels. Some had to receive an average of one to four visitors per day. Three children had to receive more than seven visitors a day.

Sexually exploited children received between D50,000 and D500,000 a day, depending on the number and type of visitors (foreigners tended to pay more). Ninety-three per cent of the children received this income. Only three girls aged 16 to 17 (7 per cent) had incomes of over D500,000. In addition, some children only made between D5,000 and D10,000 a day. The income the children made was not all theirs to keep, as 30-50 per cent of their income was given to their master and other persons such as pimps, decoys and inter-mediaries. Furthermore, almost half of them sent money home on a fairly consistent basis.

Pornographic films and lack of education were found to be the major contributing factors to sexual abuse. Although pornography is not a major problem in Viet Nam, it exists and was the cause of one instance of sexual abuse in this research. For the most part, both the victim and the law-breaker had low levels of education, especially in the remote regions of Viet Nam.

Sexual abuse is often a well-hidden secret and bears grave conse-quences for both the victim and society. After one or two violations, the victimized child often feels too ashamed to say anything and is usually threatened in order to keep the ordeal quiet. If there is no speedy consolation from family and friends, the child will sometimes, out of despair, leave home at a young age and be seduced into prostitution.

In relation to sexual exploitation, the research findings thus pointed to four major factors leading to sexual exploitation of children: sexual exploitation of children being a prosperous business; unfavourable family situation; lack of awareness about laws and appropriate sexual relations; and the changing culture and economics of Viet Nam. Details on each factors are provided below.

The sexual exploitation of children is a prosperous business. For many people involved in the process, including the law-breaking client, the brothel mistresses and the pimps. The most important contributing factor that maintains the industry of child sexual exploitation is the economic benefits from trading children and owning brothels. Though violators may be caught and imprisoned for their crime, the high economic profit leads them to carry on the business as soon as they are released. For pimps and traffickers, the economic benefit varies. They can receive as little as US$20 and as much as US$1000 to US$2000. Pimps, traffickers, and brothel mistresses or masters are most often people of low social standing: drunkards, opium smokers, lazy at work or jobless. The business of trading children does not require much investment and therefore they are easily drawn into it. There are other people who also benefit economically from trading children and their sexual exploitation: for example, mountain guides may receive D20,000 to D30,000 to lead one child through a mountainous track and across a national border.

Unfavourable family situation. Almost all the girls interviewed who had been sold into or engaged in prostitution were born to poor families: their parents had little education, their work was unstable and the family was often not united. Lack of family care seemed to contribute to the existence and increase of sexual abuse and sexual exploitation. In such family situations, children often left school early to earn a living or to contribute to the family's income. As adults, children also wanted money to spend: to eat, to play and to dress smartly, sometimes beyond the economic capacity of their families. To answer those needs and wants, the underprivileged children interviewed in the research were ready to do what was necessary to earn as much money as possible.

Lack of awareness about laws and appropriate sexual relations. The low educational levels of both parents and children (and in the case of the child, inexperience of life) made them easy prey to sexual abuse and sexual exploitation. They were often unaware of the physiological, emotional and psychological dangers of early sexual involvement and multiple partners. Further, because of limited knowledge, both adults and children alike were not cognizant of the laws of protection and judgement: victims did not report or accuse law-breakers of their crimes. There was also the misconception among both the rich and poor families (but poorly educated) that having sexual relations with a child (a virgin) would save them from contracting HIV/AIDS.

Changing culture and economics of Viet Nam. The new market economy poses many changes for Viet Nam society and it is a time of adjustment. With the incremental growth of major cities has come the immigration of children. With the transition of work, there has been greater focus on economic profit and along with this, at times, the devaluation of people. There has also been a greater influx of materials and publications (reviews and magazines, films etc.) from all kinds of different sources, some being very harmful (i.e. pornography) to the welfare of children.

(b) Factors affecting physical health

Sexual abuse and sexual exploitation had deteriorating effects on the interviewed children's physical and mental health. The physical consequences included suffering from STDs, HIV and gynaecological diseases, pregnancy and abortion.

On average, children working in a brothel were required to entertain three to seven visitors a day. If the children did not comply with the mistress or visitor, they were often beaten. On account of their sexual relations with many persons, a high proportion of sexually exploited children were infected with various diseases, including STDs, HIV and gynaecological diseases (70 per cent). The percentage of physical illness is higher in the countryside than in the towns (75 per cent in the countryside, 67 per cent in the towns). Of the sexually exploited children interviewed, 5 per cent had contracted HIV. However, it is not possible to establish precisely how many children have been infected or how many people they have infected, 70 per cent of the interviewed girls indicated that they usually used condoms when they had sexual relations. The main reason for not doing so in their sexual relations was because the customer would not use a condom.

(c) Factors affecting psychosocial health

The main problems with the children's psychosocial health included low self-esteem, symptoms of psychological stress, rejection from their families, being stigmatized by society, a dislike of men and experiencing difficulty in continuing a normal life.

A third of the children in prostitution were drug users, mainly heroine and cannabis, 16 to 17 years. They used the money they made from their customers to buy their drugs. The main reason leading to drug use was peer pressure. In addition, among children enduring sexual abuse and sexual exploitation, the investigation showed that 12 girls had become pregnant. However, only four had remained pregnant to bear the child, while the others have had abortions. Abortions are very dangerous to the life and health of young girls under age, apart from the fact that having an abortion in the period of development can lead to infertility.

Furthermore, children were constantly obsessed by the fear of being beaten and scolded by brothel mistresses and pimps. Psychologically, especially in the case of those having been sold to sex establishments, normally they had lost confidence in others. The result is that many of the girls hated men, as they were looked upon by them as mere objects to satisfy their sexual appetites.

The investigation into children enduring abuse for commercial aims shows that many of them suffer from symptoms of mental illness such as fear (48.8 per cent), anger (14.29 per cent), shame (19.7 per cent), despair (14.29 per cent), and apathy (12.32 per cent). In addition, the majority of the sexually exploited children suffered from diseases of the sexual organs.[7]

Another consequence of sexual abuse and sexual exploitation is the negative stigma that is attached to the child; this has an impact on the child's self esteem and ultimately on the child's future opportunities and acceptance in society. In Viet Nam, commercial sex workers are despised and looked down upon with contempt. People call them whores and avoid them. This makes it very difficult for sexually exploited children to be reintegrated into their community. The interviewed sexually exploited children indicated that they wanted to learn a trade and receive hospital treatment so that they could escape from sexual exploitation, and become simple labourers like other people. However, their aspiration to lead a common life was difficult to realize as so many social prejudices and opinions existed against them. The children who suffered sexual abuse from persons of the same sex were very much aware of the abnormality of their situation and did not think much about the future. Rather, they only thought of earning a lot of money and leading a happy life with their friends when not entertaining their "visitors". This could possibly be viewed as a form of escapism for the children or perhaps a way of surviving when they were not offered alternative lifestyles.

For the interviewed children who endured sexual abuse, their strongest desire was the punishment of law-breakers and the prevention of further sexual abuse. They longed for the protection of children and of the whole society from the crude actions by abusers. They also desired appropriate compensation for the crime committed against them so that their family could take care of their health.

---

[7] Nguyen Xuan Qua "A few ideas on the solution of girls and women trade in provinces of the South", report submitted at the Conference of Prevention against Women Trade in South and Centre Provinces, 27-29 September 1997.

(d) Available services/gaps in services

In the interviewed cases where the children were sexually abused on one occasion, there were several ways in which the abuse was exposed and stopped. One was when the child told the parents, and the other was when the child began to act as if he or she were terrified. Sometimes, after the first incident of sexual abuse took place, the law-breakers chose to discontinue (23 per cent). In the cases where the victim's family discovered the abuse, the perpetrator was confronted and the abuse stopped (15 per cent). However, sometimes children were too frightened to say anything to their family and this was when they were vulnerable to repeated violations.

The research findings showed that children enduring sexual abuse and sexual exploitation were often assisted with their medical needs. Medical attention was of great concern to the children themselves. Children who suffered sexual exploitation were taken to medical centres for examination by those working for social organizations. Expenses for medical examinations and care at a provincial and district hospital were a great problem. Fifty per cent of the interviewed sexually exploited children had free medical inspections, whereas the others had to pay the expenses. For 20 per cent of the study cases, it was the child's family who paid the expenses of medical examination and treatment for which many would then receive compensation from the molesters or their families through the intervention of authorities. Houses of Affection and Centres have provided social assistance.

In general, children were examined and treated at provincial or district hospitals and/or at neighbourhood infirmaries and social protection centres of the DOLISA Office. At the social protection centres, sexually abused and sexually exploited children received both medical treatment and health and emotional counselling. However, it is important to bear in mind that inspection and examination do not necessarily include treatment. In fact, most medical facilities are limited in being able to provide all that is needed to treat sexually abused and sexually exploited children effectively as they are not specialized in servicing children in these specific conditions.

There are also numerous social organizations that visit and encourage poor families, find shelters for wandering children and help train them for employment. Further, contrary to the common belief that the police are involved in exploiting children, many children enduring sexual exploitation are found by police and taken to centres of social protection. It is in these centres that children are assisted and receive vocational training. Only a few children are found to enter

Houses of Affection, Open House, etc. of their own free will. Most often they stay on the streets until they are found or caught by the police.

Children benefit greatly from protection centres where they learn a vocational skill, are assisted in finding a job, kept from loitering on the streets and find themselves in a community of children who can empathize with them. Apart from being freed from sexual abuse and sexual exploitation, they receive financial assistance, emotional or moral support, consolation and encouragement from their family, friends, the government and the police. Furthermore, at times the violators of the children are caught. Last but not least, medical organizations assist them by taking care of their health.

In Viet Nam, the Government, as well as international non-governmental organizations, provide services to sexually abused and sexually exploited children and youth. The research study found eight Vietnamese organizations that contribute to the prevention of sexual abuse and exploitation of children: the Committee for the Care and Protection of Children, with a system in place of taking care and fostering children in different localities; the Department of Social Evils Prevention, with its system of centres for social protection in various localities; clinics and hospitals; the Vietnamese Women's Union; the police; the Court of Investigation; the Tribunal, and border forces (in border provinces). The yearly budget of these organizations (including the state budget, and foreign and home assistance) towards the prevention of sexual abuse and sexual exploitation is not large. The number of organizations having an yearly budget of over D100 million accounts for only 50 per cent of the organizations examined in the research.

Efforts towards the elimination and prevention of sexual abuse and sexual exploitation are somewhat new in Viet Nam. Most of the organizations researched by the field group have participated in this domain for only four or five years. Only 50 per cent of the organizations investigated were found to have carried out preventative activities for more than five years. There is not yet a government branch particularly specialized in this activity, even though there has been an increase in the proportion of children enduring sexual abuse and sexual exploitation in recent years.

Staff working in organizations researched by the team, interested in the care and prevention of sexually abused and sexually exploited children are normally middle-aged, between 30 and 49 years, and most of them are women. More than 70 per cent of the personnel working in these organizations receive a salary and the majority have gone through some sort of short or long training course in a field of specialized study. Thirty-one per cent of the cadres receiving a salary hold a university or post-graduate degree. Training specialities include management, economics, sociology, medicine and pedagogy (this accounts for 72 per cent of the organizations identified in the research). Ninety-one per cent of the service workers had salaries of less than D500,000 per month. About 38 per cent of the salaried workers received a salary of under D300,000 per month. Although their monthly income is low compared to other social cadres, it is out of their love and concern for sexually abused and sexually exploited children that workers continue to work for these organizations.

In general, the research showed that governmental and non-governmental organizations were aiding children subject to sexual abuse and sexual exploitation. Sexually exploited children were assisted in buying their food, in learning, in apprenticeship programmes, and in finding employment. Some organizations, such as three in Hanoi, one in Da Nang, and one in Can Tho, were able to give financial assistance to the families of victims.

One example is the Committee for the Care and Protection of Children in Ho Chi Minh City, which has many programmes for assisting children, including care for children's health; care for their cultural life; care for their education; and care for children in difficult situations, including those enduring sexual abuse and sexual exploitation, and street children. Ho Chi Minh City also has a plan for administering lodgings for wandering children. In addition, there exist other organizations assisting the children, such as Houses of Affection, Open Houses, Warm Roof etc.

The present challenge is the unification of these centres in regard to management, personnel formation and training in order to increase the capacity of the staff so that the assistance provided to the target group can be more effective. Many cadres and personnel at various bases have not been trained (except cadres of DOLISA branches) and have become involved simply out of their concern for children.

According to the observations carried out in the social and health service facilities, the majority of the organizations had a waiting room and a boarding house and received children from other organizations. However, only 30 per cent of the organizations had relatively sufficient resources to meet the demands. For many organizations, there was need for social and medical personnel having professional training along with the necessary medical equipment.

A number of organizations, such as the House of Affection, the Open House and Centres for Social Protection have been established to receive sexually abused and sexually exploited children in residences for rehabilitation. However, the living conditions and the accessibility to the needed materials, equipment and personnel is very much a felt need in most of these centres. Social cadres hope that there will soon be greater assistance from organizations at home and abroad for the improvement of these centres and rehabilitation programmes.

(e) Case studies

The following is a case where the girl's parents divorced.

My parents have divorced and nobody pays attention to me. I have no one on whom I can rely. At first, I followed my friend to work and was hired at coffee-bar No 6 on Dong Tam Street. I received an income of D200,000 per month. After a while, a person encouraged me to work in another place where I was promised I would make more money. I accepted. However, I did not know that I had been sold at the price of D500,000 to a brothel. Since then, I have been entertaining visitors. (Department of Social Evils Prevention: a case study in Hanoi on 3 July 1998.)

In the following example, an orphan girl was sold to a brothel master by her lover.

H. is 16 years old and she lost her parents during her childhood. Living with her brother and sister-in-law in the countryside, she had to work hard, but was beaten, severely scolded and cursed. She left the house and went with her lover to Hanoi. Then her lover deceived her and sold her to a brothel mistress when she was 14 years old. She was sold many times and went through many masters. Normally, she had to welcome and entertain six to seven guests a day, and on some days she entertained 10 visitors. Once she had to welcome and entertain five visitors at the same time. Homeless and jobless, she has no other choice. Now she lives at the Centre of Social Protection No. II of Hanoi, in the hope of finding a job after leaving the Centre (Department of Social Evils Prevention: a case study in Hanoi on 3 July 1998).

The following is the case study of a girl suffering grave physical and emotional consequences from sexual abuse and exploitation.

She was sexually violated by her boyfriend. He then cheated her by selling her to a brothel mistress. She became a prostitute. After 409 days, her father found her and took her home. He found her in a coma-like state after having drunk too many soporific substances. Though she had been rescued, she still struggles with physical diseases. Not only are her sexual organs gravely inflamed but she is always sad and despondent. Perhaps she has been infected with HIV from all her sexual relations (five or six customers per day) as the visitors did not use condoms. Neither her parents nor the girl wanted to speak of this matter. Her father constantly says in pain: I have lost a child. (Department of Social Evils Prevention: a case study in Hanoi on 3 July 1998).

Chapter V

Conclusions and Recommendations

A. CONCLUSIONS

Sexual abuse and sexual exploitation of children and youth exist in varying degrees in all countries in the Greater Mekong Subregion. They are extremely sensitive topics in all the participating countries of the subregion and the fact that the current project is being undertaken in these countries in collaboration with government departments (in all countries except Cambodia, where the national coordinating organization is a local NGO) indicates that there is recognition of the existence of the phenomenon and the will to take action. However, because of the taboo attached to both sexual abuse and sexual exploitation of children and youth, and its criminal nature, it is difficult to collect accurate data. The following conclusions can thus be made from the six national studies.

1. Availability of data

Secondary data on sexual abuse of children and youth is difficult to locate because there has been a lack of research in this field thus far, and few cases are reported to officials. The children often do not disclose the crime and adults do not believe the child when they do so. In many cases, monetary compensation was paid to the family of the abused child instead of reporting to the police. Many children and youth also did not know the definition of sexual abuse and sexual exploitation and thus it was impossible for them and their families to report such cases to the authorities. This was found to be particularly prevalent among ethnic minority populations and in rural areas that have proved difficult to target under past education and awareness-raising campaigns. In relation to sexual exploitation of children and youth, data were found to be more available and complete in Cambodia and Thailand, where groups have been active against the phenomenon for a longer period. These are also countries with an extensive market for children in prostitution, with both countries acting as demand and supply countries for children in prostitution within the subregion. All countries of the subregion lacked a systematic method of collecting and managing information related to sexual abuse and sexual exploitation of children.

2. Policies and legislation

Provisions relating to sexual abuse and sexual exploitation of children and youth exist in the criminal and penal codes of all six countries but, with the exception of Thailand, a comprehensive policy and specific legislation to address sexual abuse and sexual exploitation do not exist. However, the main problem does not seem to lie with the lack of specific policies and laws to protect the children but rather the implementation of existing laws. Lack of law enforcement was found to result from the lack of legal knowledge as well as the lack of sufficient cooperation between government and non-governmental organizations and between different governmental organizations in addressing these issues in some countries; in other countries it was reported that lack of law enforcement resulted from the involvement of police and military officers in the prostitution and trafficking of children.

3. Causes of sexual abuse

The data on sexual abuse of children were more complete from the study carried out in Thailand, and therefore the following conclusions are based on the findings from Thailand. At the individual level, biological factors, including developmental disability, played a major role in children's vulnerability to sexual abuse. Children with disabilities were unable to protect themselves from the offender and, in severe cases of developmental disability, the child was dependent on the sexual offender. At the family level, poverty, child neglect, family breakdown and dysfunction were other factors found to contribute to sexual abuse of children. Substance abuse among adults in the family and psychiatric illness were other contributing factors. At the community level, an unsafe school environment was found to increase children's vulnerability to sexual abuse. In addition, punitive (jail and fines) measures that existed to deal with sexual offenders in all countries of the subregion often did not deter sexual abusers from repeating their crimes.

4. Causes of sexual exploitation

Several factors at the individual, family and community/societal levels made children extremely vulnerable to sexual exploitation in all the six countries. At the individual level, illiteracy, low levels of education and lack of vocational training prevented children from acquiring well-paying jobs, which caused them to rely on prostitution for income. Other available employment options, such as working in factories, were too difficult and the salaries were low. Ignorance on the part of the children made it easy for people to lure them to work in the sex industry. Other factors that made young people vulnerable to sexual exploitation included lack of awareness about the Convention on the Rights of the Child and the health effects of commercial sex work, history of sexual abuse and premarital sexual relations. Children with a history of sexual abuse were especially vulnerable as their experience made them feel hopeless and depressed, particularly because most of them felt that they had no future owing to the traditional attitudes upheld in all countries of the subregion regarding the sanctity of virginity before marriage. Street children and youth were another high-risk group for sexual exploitation, as some were forced to sell their sexual services in order to earn enough money to meet their basic needs.

At the family level, the research results from the six countries indicate that low educational level, poverty and family dysfunction were the major factors contributing to children working in the commercial sex sector. Children and youth from poor families supplemented their parent's income by working in prostitution, as the income generated was high. In other instances, children and youth entered prostitution because they felt unloved and neglected by their parents who were working hard to survive, were divorced or were abusing substances. In cases where a child had been sexually abused by a family member, running away from home was the only way to avoid further abuse. These children often ended up in prostitution.

Rural poverty and rapid urban growth were identified as two key factors at the community level which contributed to children's vulnerability to sexual exploitation. Lack of adequate facilities, including sports centres in the rural areas, made young people vulnerable to substance abuse and sexual exploitation as they lacked opportunities to use their free time in a constructive way. On the other hand, rapid urban growth enticed children from rural areas to migrate to the cities, but without adequate vocational skills they could not find lucrative jobs and thus ended up working in the sex industry. Lack of sexual health education, the availability of pornographic films, and the presence of sex establishments and traffickers in the communities were also factors that made children vulnerable to sexual exploitation. The study showed that several members of the community were involved in the trafficking of children and youth into prostitution through false promises of jobs as maids and helpers in the cities where they were often sold to brothels. Young people from minority groups entered prostitution because their communities, including their family, accepted it and encouraged them to do so, in some cases to satisfy materialistic desires. Another contributing factor was the demand for virgins and the high price paid for such girls in all countries of the subregion. A lack of awareness about the Convention on the Right of the Child and state laws on sexual abuse and sexual exploitation of children also existed among the general public, and concerned officials lacked the proper incentives to abide by the Convention and laws. The studies also indicated that the caregivers in many of the organizations working with sexually abused and sexually exploited children lacked the knowledge and skills required to provide these children with appropriate care. This resulted in some of the sexually exploited children running away from the caregivers and returning to prostitution.

5. Health effects

The sexually abused and sexually exploited children interviewed in the countries of the subregion had numerous health problems, from sexually transmitted infections, urinary problems and unwanted pregnancy, to poor school performance, substance abuse, mental illness and suicidal behaviour. Both sexual abuse and sexual exploitation had devastating effects on a child's sense of identity and sexuality and on his or her capacity to build relationships. They often caused low self-esteem in the victims. Victims of sexual abuse had a high probability of entering prostitution because they did not receive timely help and healing for their traumas. It was noted in some places, including Yunnan Province (China) and Viet Nam, that children who had been sexually abused prior to entering prostitution tended to have the most severe psychosocial problems, including self-mutilation and suicidal behaviour.

6. Available social and health services

In all countries in the subregion there was a lack of services and training for staff in the existing health and social services. In some, such as the Lao People's Democratic Republic and Myanmar, and in

Yunnan Province (China), there were no specific or specialized programmes to address the health needs of sexually abused and sexually exploited children. There were programmes that worked directly with the target group in Cambodia, Thailand and Viet Nam but in Cambodia those tended to be concentrated in the capital city. Moreover, many of the existing organizations which served sexually abused and sexually exploited children conducted emergency work and they did not have the capacity to carry out effective rehabilitation. In Viet Nam, the services were provided by government agencies, while in Cambodia and Thailand these programmes tended to be the domain of the NGO and religious sector. The lack of services and adequate training among staff has meant that evidence of sexual abuse and sexual exploitation among children was often overlooked or went unaddressed. Moreover, an inability to speak openly about the sexual abuse of children signified that these children will not receive the required medical care. Access to proper medical care by sexually exploited children was also limited owing to the criminality of prostitution and substance abuse and the social stigma attached to people living with HIV/AIDS. The overwhelming majority of sexually exploited children treated illnesses at the local pharmacy.

In addition, police and court procedures still put the weight of the legal process on the child and his or her family to prove that the abuse occurred. Through lengthy legal procedures, during which the child would be living in the same house or community as the offender, many victims were essentially re-abused. That discouraged reporting and also resulted in only a small percentage of cases being resolved legally.

The studies also showed that the majority of sexually exploited children wished to leave the brothel and be trained in vocational and business skills, but such opportunities were not readily available in all countries of the subregion. Prior to entering prostitution, they did not possess the skills necessary to find alternative forms of gainful employment.

7. Reintegration

The studies indicated that some of the sexually abused children and many of the sexually exploited children were unable to be fully reintegrated into their communities. Sexually abused children were rejected by society and in several cases, as a result became children in prostitution. Sexually exploited children also suffered from social stigmatization and thus found it difficult to reintegrate into society.

B. RECOMMENDATIONS: WHAT NEEDS TO BE DONE?

The recommendations that follow are based on the findings from
the research that was conducted in the six participating countries and
from feedback received from the national HRD workshops for social
and health care providers held upon the completion of the research.
The workshops were intended both to disseminate the results from the
research and to elicit input for formulating additional recommendations
and developing the training curriculum and pilot projects. The recommendations are grouped under three levels of prevention: primary,
secondary and tertiary. Specific recommendations are also made with
regard to training and future research. More detailed country recommendations are contained in annex I.

Interventions at **the primary level of prevention** suggest
programmes that will promote a safe and healthy environment in
which all children and youth can grow without fear of sexual abuse
and sexual exploitation. The main features of primary prevention
include specific policies and laws, basic health, education and housing
services, and the provision of information and education through a
variety of channels. Policies and legislation can have a powerful
impact on the conditions that promote healthy development in young
people. It is important that such policies and laws be integrated,
taking into account the many different sectors that affect the healthy
development of children. The strength of basic health, education and
housing services and the amount of appropriate attention they can give
to children depend in large measure on national priorities as expressed
through policies and legislation. The public, including children and
youth, can be informed of issues related to sexual abuse and sexual
exploitation of children and youth by means of one-way channels of
communication, such as radio, television, live entertainment, newspa-
pers, magazines, books, comics, cartoons, videos, films, cassettes,
records, posters or pamphlets, or through two-way communication –
in person, by telephone, or through an exchange of written messages.
Interactive communication is especially powerful, since it permits
people to ask questions and explore issues of special individual signifi-
cance, ensuring that the information has a greater degree of personal
relevance. Education not only provides information for children and
youth but also nurtures intellectual as well as social and moral
development. Education should not only include guidance on matura-
tion, sexuality and relationships but also aim at enabling children to
manage their own healthy destiny. The two major vehicles for such
education are the school system, which often provides formal training
in sexual health education, and the family, the primary source of
knowledge and habit formation for everyone. Other people who can

play a significant role in providing education to children and youth are health workers, leaders of youth organizations, religious leaders, modern heroes of sport and entertainment and so on. For education to be a success, educators must be both knowledgeable and skilled at communicating with the public and the young, in particular. This means being able to listen sensitively and without condemning the individual.

The interventions at the **secondary level of prevention** are meant to identify vulnerable groups of children and reduce the risk of sexual abuse and sexual exploitation. Research, including that under-taken by ESCAP, has shown that some children and youth are more vulnerable than others to sexual abuse and sexual exploitation because of their individual, family or social circumstances. Programmes at this level of prevention therefore are typically grass-roots-oriented, relying on key institutions such as the family, school, church, village council, health centre, social or youth club, women's group, and so on, for initial identification and action. However, because many schools and communities are without an effective screening service, self-reporting and identification by family or community groups long after the sexual abuse and/or sexual exploitation has taken place is more common. Secondary prevention will only be effective if young people in need are reached early enough with sex education and life skills training to increase their resilience. In many countries in the subregion, children often do not know where to turn or what help can be provided. It is a major challenge to make services and service providers more accessible to the young. If public information on sexual abuse and sexual exploitation is readily available, in and out of school, and accurate, it is more likely that children will seek care when they need it. For this to work well in the long term, it requires a two-way process in which the local institutions identify and contact the children at risk of sexual abuse and sexual exploitation and, at the same time, the child is willing to trust, confide in and seek out those who can help him or her. People with the ability to listen well, who feel and show respect for the individual child, are more likely to attract children seeking help, whether they are in a professional setting or not.

Tertiary prevention aims to reduce harm or further damage to child victims of sexual abuse or sexual exploitation. The main focus is on compensatory services for those in fluid situations, treatment and (re)habilitation. A key element in tertiary prevention is the avail-ability and accessibility of counselling, treatment and rehabilitation services for physical, mental and social problems. Treatment and rehabilitation can focus on the individual, family or community and can be carried out in an institutional setting or on an outreach basis. The approach that is selected depends on the careful examination of the child and his or her family and community. Complications can be prevented or cured much more easily if the child and his or her immediate family understand the problem and if those who provide the care are aware of the special needs and perceptions of sexually abused and sexually exploited children and their families. Services that treat such children and youth are largely in the health and social welfare sectors and have great variation. They are predominantly aimed at physical and social problems and, to a lesser extent, at problems of mental health. The few services available in the health and social sectors appear to be curative and stigmatizing respectively. Providing care early to prevent more chronic conditions is highly cost-effective. Furthermore, rehabilitation needs to be directed at the whole individual so that he or she is able to develop physically, psychologically and socially to the fullest extent possible. This requires good cooperation between the sectors, particularly between health, education and social services, and the involvement of community and non-governmental organizations. The efforts must be directed not only at the young person, but also at those who have contact with him or her, and this calls for retraining and awareness-training for health and social service personnel so that they are better equipped to help the child integrate into his or her natural setting. When a prolonged stay in a hospital or rehabilitation institution is necessary, efforts must be made to maintain a normal environment as far as possible, including, for example, continued schooling, association with peers, recreation, and daily chores compatible with age and recovery, so as to help psychosocial and physical development and pave the way for a return to normality.

The Human Resources Development Section of ESCAP is aware of the challenges that the participating six countries of the subregion now face to turn their recommendations into action. It is also aware of the fact that governments in the respective countries must initiate such action. In its effort to further strengthen the capacity of government agencies and NGOs responsible for programmes targeting sexually abused and sexually exploited children and youth in the subregion, ESCAP has implemented the following activities.

(a) Established a web site, which is available to countries in the Greater Mekong Subregion. The web site provides detailed information about the current situation of sexual abuse and sexual exploitation of children and youth in the countries of the subregion, legislation to protect children from sexual abuse and sexual exploitation, information on complementary activities under way in the context of the subregion and their relationship to other regional and international initiatives. It also includes a directory of organizations in countries of the subregion engaged in programmes to prevent or combat sexual abuse and sexual exploitation of children. The national coordinating organizations collaborating with ESCAP in this project will continue to serve as focal points for each participating country and will be responsible for providing information to the web site. Moreover, a video depicting the situation of sexually abused and sexually exploited children in the subregion has been developed and distributed to the participating countries to create more awareness of the phenomenon.

(b) The conduct of a subregional course in September 2000 to provide training that will help social and health-care professionals in the subregion to deal with the needs and problems of sexually abused and sexually exploited children. The course will also address caregivers' needs and how to deal with them, as well as equip them with a child-centred approach in carrying out needs assessments, planning programmes, implementing, monitoring and evaluating programmes for sexually abused and sexually exploited children.

The above-mentioned activities that are being implemented by ESCAP will invariably strengthen exchange and collaboration within countries of the subregion to prevent sexual abuse and sexual exploitation of children and youth and facilitate the repatriation and reintegration of young people who have been trafficked within and across borders. It could also form the basis for exchange visits, joint research and investigation on both preventive and remedial approaches.

Finally, ESCAP is aware that the shortage or ineffective allocation of funds is one of the main obstacles to the delivery of services to sexually abused and sexually exploited children and youth. To this end, ESCAP will continue to work with governments and NGOs to stress the importance of the provision of health and social services to victims of sexual abuse and sexual exploitation. ESCAP will also work in partnership with governments and NGOs to implement follow-up projects targeting sexually abused and sexually exploited children and youth, and the conduct of national training courses on service provision.

Annexes

Annex I: Recommendations from country reports

The following recommendations are especially pertinent to government and non-governmental programmes in the six countries of the subregion participating in this research project. The following abbreviations are used in the recommendations: primary prevention (PP), secondary prevention (SP), tertiary prevention (TP), research (R), and training (T).

A. CAMBODIA

Recommendations from the research

(1) The quality and delivery of basic health and education services need to be improved in order that all citizens, particularly children, can access them, including those who live in rural areas (PP).

(2) Existing laws to protect children from sexual abuse and sexual exploitation should be enforced by the police and other government officers in a smooth, open and coordinated manner. Sexually exploited children should be treated as victims and not criminals (PP).

(3) Awareness-raising activities on the implications and consequences of sexual abuse and sexual exploitation of children should be conducted in high-risk communities. Networks, which exist to eliminate the sexual exploitation of children, should be strengthened (SP).

(4) The activities in recommendation No. 3 should be combined with vocational training courses, revolving funds and employment to enable children as well as their parents to learn skills and have alternative sources of income (SP).

(5) More centres should be established to provide shelter, medical care, counselling and skills training for sexually abused and sexually exploited children, particularly in those provinces in which these services do not currently exist and in those with high concentrations of children in prostitution (TP).

(6) Innovative outreach services are needed to address the physical and psychological health needs of sexually exploited children (TP).

(7) Sexually exploited children who are kept against their will in brothels should be released (TP).

(8) Awareness-raising activities should be conducted to reduce societal discrimination against sexually abused and sexually exploited children (TP).

(9) Law enforcers should be trained to change their attitudes and behaviour regarding sexually abused and sexually exploited children. Brothel owners should receive training in the prevention of STDs, including HIV/AIDS. Caregivers who work with sexually abused and sexually exploited children, and with vulnerable children in general, lack the skills required to provide them with appropriate psychological care. These staff members need to be trained to be able to identify the psychological needs of sexually abused and sexually exploited children, who are often traumatized children, as well as the skills to address those needs (T).

(10) Both qualitative and quantitative studies should be conducted on the sexual abuse of children in Cambodia, as there is a lack of research in this field thus far. Children with disabilities should be included in the focus of the study (R).

Additional recommendations from the national HRD workshop held at Phnom Penh from 2 to 4 June 1999

(11) Education and public awareness should be heightened with regard to HIV/AIDS (PP).

(12) Collaboration between government organizations and NGOs working to assist sexually abused and sexually exploited children should be strengthened (SP).

(13) A referral system, including medical care centres, counselling and psychosocial services, and skilled psychologists should be established to handle cases of sexually abused and sexually exploited children (TP).

(14) Substance abuse problems among sexually exploited children should be addressed (TP).

B. Yunnan Province (China)

Recommendations from the research

(1) Sex education should be included in the school curriculum, and public awareness of sexual issues, particularly sexual health, should be increased (PP).

(2) Existing laws and regulations should be reinforced and fully implemented, while new legislation needs to be put in place to ensure the protection of the rights and interests of women, children and youth, particularly with regard to curbing the commercial sex trade, trafficking in women and children, pornography and other forms of sexual exploitation (PP).

(3) Steps must be taken to promote sexual equality in both the social and the legal aspects (PP).

(4) Knowledge of STDs and AIDS must be disseminated through various channels, in order to raise public awareness of these diseases. In particular, this information must be made available to those involved in the commercial sex trade, who are more difficult to access because of the covert nature of their work (SP).

(5) Measures should be taken to help women, children and youth who have been involved in the commercial sex trade, or who are victims of sexual abuse, to increase their levels of self-esteem. Negative social attitudes towards these groups must also be addressed. Social workers and family members can also be trained to provide advice on relevant laws, as well as on sexual matters, in order to reach those women, children and youth who have not had access to government programmes (SP).

(6) Community-based work must to be conducted as a means of assisting sexually exploited and sexually abused youth and children, and to prevent others from being involved (TP).

(7) When designing community-based action, measures must be taken and implemented in relation to the situation prevailing in each area. For example, a profile of women's and children's social and economic development can be drawn up in an area where there is a considerable amount of trafficking in women, and comprehensive development projects based on these findings can be established. These development projects should incorporate programmes to enhance the protection of the rights and interests of women and children, programmes of education for female children, and promotion of fertility and health (TP).

(8) Training programmes should be developed aimed at raising awareness of AIDS and STDs, and their prevention (TP).

(9) More education is required on the legal and personal rights of women, in order to provide more women with knowledge of how laws can be used in circumstances where their personal rights have been violated, or are under threat. Legal assistance, psychological counselling and information on health must be provided for sexually abused women and children, to ensure that their personal rights will not be violated again (TP).

(10) Community-based organizations should develop their capacity to prevent the trafficking of women and children (TP).

(11) Close attention must be paid to saving and helping the most vulnerable groups of women, and to providing assistance, medical treatment, legal aid and psychological counselling to women, children and youth who have been rescued from situations of abuse and/or exploitation (TP).

(12) Training courses to develop women's vocational skills must be provided, in order to equip them with the means to achieve a stable livelihood (TP).

(13) Training courses should be provided for family members and social workers in communities with a high incidence of entry into the commercial sex trade. The trainees should be asked to raise awareness about legal matters, sexuality and health, as well as provide ideological counselling for those children and youth who have been involved, or are at risk of involvement, in commercial sex work (TP).

(14) Information on sexual issues and sexual health should be made available in communities where cases of sexual abuse are common, in order to reduce the number of cases of sexual abuse (TP).

(15) The sexually exploited and sexually abused children need assistance in reintegrating into their home communities and families to minimize personal trauma as much as possible, as well as developing life goals and resuming normal lives (TP).

(16) The youth and children who are reluctant to return to their former careers after their release from the detention centre, or refuse to continue to engage in the pornographic trades should be given practical assistance in the areas of employment, study, training, marriage, housing and family relations, so that they will not be forced to go back to, or become trapped in, commercial sex work (T).

(17) Girl prostitutes who go on with their careers should also be advised on how to protect themselves, so as to reduce the risk of contracting STDs; for those girl prostitutes who have been detained, the training programmes should incorporate sexual education, health education, training in technical skills, and education on legal issues (T).

(18) More attention needs to be paid to the provision of psychological counselling for these groups (T).

(19) Family education and marriage adjustment training should be conducted among the parents or husbands of these girl prostitutes so that they can enter a favourable family environment after their release from the detention centre (T).

(20) The sexually exploited and sexually abused children need training courses which provide knowledge of hygiene and health, particularly basic knowledge of the spread and prevention of STDs and HIV/AIDS (T).

C. Lao People's Democratic Republic

(1) Existing laws relating to sexual abuse and sexual exploitation should be reviewed and improved to protect children more adequately, and public awareness should be raised among the general public on these laws. Additional laws to protect children should also be formulated, including those that prohibit children from entering entertainment establishments (PP).

(2) Children, at high risk of sexual exploitation should be trained in appropriate vocations. Particular attention should be paid to juvenile delinquents, drop-outs and other marginalized children (SP).

(3) The working conditions of factories, including garment factories, should be improved (SP).

(4) A sex education curriculum should be developed and taught in schools with a specific component on sexual abuse and sexual exploitation (SP).

(5) Parents should be actively involved in raising their children and decreasing their vulnerability to sexual abuse and sexual exploitation (SP).

(6) Organizations should be established to provide services to sexually abused and sexually exploited children, including counselling, rehabilitation and medical services. Existing government health facilities should be upgraded to offer such services. These services should be accessible to sexually abused and sexually exploited children (TP).

(7) Existing and potential care providers should be trained, in order to address the health needs of sexually abused and sexually exploited children effectively. Possible topics for training could include statistics collection techniques; counselling children on how to protect themselves; knowledge about medical, psychological and social health issues; treatment; and implementation of appropriate vocational education programmes for youth (TP).

(8) Outreach programmes should be implemented to raise awareness among sexually exploited children on health issues, covering STDs, including HIV/AIDS; the dangers of substance abuse; and proper treatment from medical personnel, including gynaecologists (TP).

(9) Sexually exploited children should receive vocational training and they should be assisted in the search for alternative forms of employment (TP).

(10) Further research should be conducted on the physical and psychosocial needs of sexually exploited children as well as their specific health service needs, particularly in the provinces not covered by the study, such as those in the northern part of the country. Further studies should also target children of the many ethnic groups other than the Lao Loum. Sexually abused children and their health needs should also be researched. The research could be conducted with the collaboration of the Ministry of Labour and Social Welfare, the Ministry of Health and the Ministry of Interior. Half of the researchers should be women, as this research showed that sexually exploited children trusted women more than men (R).

Additional recommendations from the national HRD workshop held at Vientiane from 4 to 6 May 1999

(11) Basic health care and medical services in the country, including clinics, hospitals, pharmacies and traditional health care, should be improved, particularly in areas outside the Vientiane municipality. Some of these services should be established in all villages and districts (PP).

118

(12) Child development centres and consultation centres should be established throughout the country (PP).

(13) Public information campaigns on the health effects of substance abuse should be launched (PP).

(14) Family members and members of the community of the sexually abused and sexually exploited children should be informed on how to assist them, as well as on the services available for such children, once they are developed (PP).

D. MYANMAR

(1) Strict enforcement of the laws that exist to protect sexually abused and sexually exploited children should be strengthened through the joint efforts of governmental and non-governmental organizations. Some laws should be further elaborated in line with the Convention on the Rights of the Child (PP).

(2) The quality and accessibility of educational and health-care services in Myanmar should be improved, particularly in rural and remote areas (PP).

(3) Public awareness should be heightened concerning the Convention and its implications, particularly among children (PP).

(4) The delivery of health education should be enhanced, particularly at the village level, so that positive behavioural changes occur in addition to increased knowledge of health topics, such as personal hygiene, nutrition, reproductive health and HIV/AIDS (PP).

(5) Families should be strengthened through increased economic and social service support, particularly those in high-risk communities (SP).

(6) Rehabilitation centres for sexually abused and sexually exploited children should be established throughout the country. Existing health services for these children should be widely publicized (TP).

(7) The number of health-care facilities, including hospitals, clinics and public health care centres, should be increased and made accessible to sexually abused and sexually exploited children (TP).

(8) Awareness and understanding of the health risks of unsafe sexual relations and substance abuse should be promoted among sexually exploited children, their customers and the owners of sexual establishments, particularly in relation to the transmission of HIV/AIDS and STDs (TP).

**Additional recommendations from the
national HRD workshop held at Yangon
from 7 to 9 April 1999**

(9) Recreational facilities for children, including playgrounds, should
be built (SP).

(10) Children in high-risk communities should be provided with the
resources and training needed to earn sufficient income (SP).

(11) Sexual abuse should be discussed (SP).

(12) Foster parent programmes should be expanded for sexually
abused and sexually exploited children (SP).

(13) In addition to the need for establishing rehabilitation centres for
sexually abused and sexually exploited children, existing institutional services and community-based services need to be improved
(TP).

(14) The number of health facilities that conduct HIV/AIDS testing
should be increased, and existing services should be strengthened
(TP).

(15) The quantitative and qualitative data collection skills of social
workers should be developed in order to facilitate research on
sexually abused and sexually exploited children (R).

E. THAILAND

(1) The Prevention and Suppression of Prostitution Act, BE 2539
(1996), should be enforced (PP).

(2) The law regarding the closing hours of entertainment establishments and those which bar the entry of children to them should
be enforced (PP).

(3) The number of entertainment establishments should be reduced
and the remaining ones should be contained in one area (PP).

(4) Support for children at high risk of sexual abuse and sexual
exploitation should be provided so that they can continue their
education. This should be combined with appropriate vocational
training between Grades 6 and 9 (SP).

(5) Recommendation (4) should be coupled with support for the
children's parents in the form of income-generation activities for
poor families (SP).

(6) Special care should be provided to street children, including the provision of accommodation and food. The Homes should be open, allowing children to seek assistance but also giving them the freedom to stay or leave (SP).

(7) Members of the community, especially parents should be informed about the frequency at which sexual abuse and sexual exploitation occurs; they should try to ensure that their baby-sitters are not sexual abusers. Parents and other community members should be made aware of the physical and psychosocial impact of sexual abuse. They should be able to detect the need for rehabilitation in order to help their children and they should know whom to contact regarding cases of sexual abuse and sexual exploitation (SP).

(8) Parents and communities should be educated regarding the exploitation and health risks involved with prostitution, including HIV/AIDS (SP).

(9) Sports centres should be established and children should be encouraged to spend their free time playing. The centres should be equipped with adequate facilities and equipment (SP).

(10) Teachers should be trained in how to handle cases of sexual abuse and sexual exploitation and should be informed of the services available to treat sexually abused and sexually exploited children in the country (SP).

(11) More centres and homes providing services for sexually abused and sexually exploited children, particularly in the area of rehabilitation, should be established in the country (TP).

(12) Caregivers who work with sexually abused and sexually exploited children should receive further training in how to treat the psychosocial problems of such cases (TP).

(13) Services for sexually abused and sexually exploited children should be improved, especially with regard to rehabilitation (TP).

(14) Male sexually abused and sexually exploited children should be targeted for physical and psychosocial care (TP).

(15) Follow-up programmes should be implemented for sexually abused and sexually exploited children who have been discharged from centres, homes and hospitals (TP).

(16) Rehabilitation programmes should be developed and implemented for sexual offenders (TP).

(17) The reporting of cases of sexual abuse should be improved (TP).

(18) The legal process for sexually abused children should be improved and shortened in length (TP).

(19) An active network should be established in all large cities and towns to assist with cases of sexual abuse. The work of organizations that serve sexually abused and sexually exploited children should be advertised so that community members are aware of their work (TP).

F. VIET NAM

(1) The Government should formulate a specific and comprehensive national policy to prevent and combat sexual abuse and sexual exploitation of children. Such a policy should also be translated into concrete programmes (PP).

(2) To better meet the needs of sexually abused and sexually exploited children, public education and advocacy programmes about relevant laws, the rights of children, sexual abuse and sexual exploitation should be developed to encourage children and families to report instances of sexual abuse and exploitation. Such education campaigns and advocacy programmes should also be implemented in remote and border areas and, where applicable, information, education and communication material should be developed in the languages of minority ethnic groups. Furthermore, campaign messages should be developed for the different information channels to ensure that a wide range of the population is reached (PP).

(3) Sexual and reproductive health education should be incorporated in the school curriculum. Both children and care providers must be aware of these issues in order to prevent the occurrence of sexual abuse and sexual exploitation of children (PP).

(4) Articles in the Penal Law need to be reviewed. The different components of these crimes need to be specified more accurately, and the punishment should be made proportional to the severity of these crimes. In fact, there should be harsher penalties for the sexual abuse and sexual exploitation of children. In particular, more severe punishments should be stipulated by articles 113, 113a and 114, up to and including life imprisonment. In addition, the existing laws should be better enforced, and the capacity of the organizations that implement these laws should also be strengthened. Finally, an ordinance on the prevention of prostitution should be drafted and promulgated (PP).

(5) Families and children at risk should have access to vocational training courses, revolving microfinance funds and employment to enable them to learn employable skills and earn an income (SP).

(6) Sexually exploited children who are kept against their will in brothels should be rescued. The study indicated that the large majority of sexually exploited children were forced into prostitution and wished to leave the brothel to receive training in vocational and business skills. As a result, brothels that keep children against their will should be raided. The children rescued by these raids should be rehabilitated and reintegrated into their families and communities (TP).

(7) More centres should be established to provide comprehensive care to sexually exploited and sexually abused children, including medical and psychosocial care, particularly in those provinces in which these services do not currently exist and in those with a high concentration of children in prostitution. To facilitate this, existing networks should be strengthened, activities should be coordinated and information should be exchanged. Finally, these services should be provided free of charge (TP).

(8) Sexually abused and sexually exploited children should be assisted in being fully reintegrated into their communities (TP).

(9) Caregivers who work with sexually abused and sexually exploited children and with other categories of vulnerable children need to be trained and equipped with the proper skills to be able to identify the needs of these children (T).

(10) Quantitative research should be carried out to identify the root causes of sexual abuse and sexual exploitation. Additional research on related legal measures is also necessary in order to combat these causes (R).

(11) There should be additional exchanges and substantive collaboration between Viet Nam and other countries, especially those in the Greater Mekong Subregion, in order to prevent the sexual exploitation of children (subregional exchange).

(12) The relevant government agencies in Viet Nam, including the Ministry of Labour, Invalids and Social Affairs and the Ministry of Foreign Affairs, should actively seek to participate in regional seminars sponsored by international organizations for the countries in the Greater Mekong Subregion (subregional exchange).

**Additional recommendations from the
national HRD workshop held at Hanoi
from 11 to 13 May 1999**

(13) Vocational training and job-placement services should be provided to school drop-outs (SP).

(14) High-risk groups, such as street children, children from big families and children working or living close to seaside resorts, should be protected from sexual abuse and sexual exploitation (SP).

(15) Specialized agencies dealing with the legal issues of sexually abused and sexually exploited children should be established and should work closely with the police (TP).

(16) Because a high percentage of sexually abused children become sexually exploited children, it is important to break this cycle of abuse and exploitation by providing timely treatment to sexually abused children (TP).

(17) Schooling should be provided for sexually abused and sexually exploited children (TP).

(18) Psychosocial counselling services should be provided for sexually abused and sexually exploited children and their families. These services should be provided not only in urban areas but also in rural areas and at the grass-roots level (TP).

(19) Care providers should be properly trained in child development, child psychology and child health, with a particular emphasis on working with sexually abused and sexually exploited children, so that these care providers may be able to meet the psychosocial and medical needs of such children (T).

(20) Research institutes should be established that would collect and analyse statistics on sexually abused and sexually exploited children in order to provide policy recommendations for the government. These research institutes and other qualified organizations should conduct research in those provinces of Viet Nam that have not been covered by the current report. Furthermore, these institutes and organizations should conduct research on children who have been sexually abused and sold into prostitution by their parents or close relatives and/or children who have been sexually exploited over a long period of time (R).

Annex II: Interview Guides
instructions for filling in the Interview Guides

There are four interview guides and one observational guide:

A. Interview Guide for project managers/coordinators: pages 1-7.

This includes questions on the organization in general, including the type and qualification of staff. There are also general questions on sexually exploited and sexually abused children and youth. Use the 'Health Inventory' as a guide to establish the most common health problems.

B. Interview Guide for health/social care providers: page 8.

Observational Guide at the health/social care facility: pages 9-11.

You should interview those who have direct contact with sexually abused and sexually exploited children and youth on a day-to-day basis in government and non-governmental programme, such as social workers, nurses, medical doctors etc. The Interview guide includes specific questions on work tasks and needs of sexually abused and sexually exploited children and youth as perceived by care givers.

Use the 'Observational Guide'. The Health Inventory should also be used as a guide to establish the most common health problems of the children and youth.

C. Interview Guide for teachers: page 12.

Contains specific questions for teachers who have direct contact with sexually abused and sexually exploited children and youth.

D. Interview Guide for children, on factors affecting health; page 13.

Interview Guide for children on factors affecting care utilization; page 14.

These Guides also include some pointers on probing a young person's background and their history of sexual abuse and/or sexual exploitation (page 15).

Use the Health Inventory to establish the health problems of the children and youth. When Questioning children, explore the use of diagramming techniques to complement verbal responses (see materials on participatory rural appraisal (PRA) methods with children).

- For each organization with direct services for sexually abused and sexually exploited children and youth, you will be required to fill in Interview Guides A, B and D. If the organization has a non-formal or vocational school, then you will also fill in C. If children attend a school situated close to the organization, find out the name of the school and the grade (class level) of most of the sexually abused and sexually exploited young people and make arrangements to interview the teachers who teach those grades/classes.

- Please write as clearly as possible, preferably in BLOCK LETTERS. If possible, enter the information into the computer at the end of each day.

- Do not be discouraged if you cannot get answers to a question. Try to get as much information as you can. Remember, in qualitative research it is the richness of the discussions that counts.

- The 'Health Inventory' requires you to fill in the number between 1 and 5, choosing one alternative from the scale provided. With service providers you should only fill in the MOST COMMON health problems of the children under their care. When using the Health Inventory with the children, however, you should fill in ALL their health problems.

- It will take, on average, 10 days to conduct interviews in one location. Interview all service providers and not more than 20 sexually abused and sexually exploited young people in each research site.

- Ask for organization publications and review these for additional information.

A. INTERVIEW GUIDE FOR PROJECT MANAGERS

NAME OF ORGANIZATION:

MAILING ADDRESS:

CONTACT PERSON/PROGRAMME:

TELEPHONE:

FAX:

E-MAIL:

TYPE OF ORGANIZATION: ☐ Governmental   ☐ Non-governmental
                         ☐ University   ☐ Hospital/Clinic
                         ☐ Religious   ☐ Other, specify

DATE OF ESTABLISHMENT:

BRANCHES/CENTRES: ☐ No   ☐ Yes (list + address)
use separate interview guides for each center

1.

2.

3.

4.

5.

ORGANIZATIONAL STRUCTURE:
(sketch on separate paper if more space required)

WORK STRUCTURE:

ANNUAL BUDGET:

BUDGET ALLOCATED TO EACH AREA OF WORK:

COMMENCEMENT OF CSEC/SA ACTIVITIES (month/year):

TOTAL NUMBER OF STAFF:
(specify number in each area of work/profession)

PREFERRED AGE OF WORKERS:
(specify area of work/profession)

PREFERRED SEX OF WORKERS:
(specify area of work/profession)

NUMBER OF PAID STAFF:
(specify number in each area of work/profession)

PROFESSION OF PAID STAFF:
(specify for each area of work/profession)

SALARY LEVEL:
(specify for each area of work/profession)

NUMBER OF VOLUNTEERS:
(specify number in each area of work/profession)

PROFESSION OF VOLUNTEERS:
(specify area of work/profession)

CRITERIA FOR SELECTION (what do they look for in their staff?):
(specify area of work/profession)

MINIMUM EDUCATIONAL QUALIFICATIONS:
(specify qualifications for area of work/profession)

MOTIVATION (what makes the workers stay):
(specify motivation for each area of work/profession)

STAFF BENEFITS (e.g. housing, transport, medical insurance):
(specify benefits for each area of work/profession)

OPPORTUNITIES FOR STAFF DEVELOPMENT
(e.g. training, supervision and support):
(specify opportunities for each area of work/profession)

SUMMARY OF WORK AND SIGNIFICANT ACHIEVEMENTS:
(ask for brochure and annual report(s) if available)

PROGRAMME OBJECTIVES:

TYPE OF SERVICES/CARE PROVIDED:

FACILITIES AVAILABLE:

NUMBER OF CHILDREN AT TIME OF INTERVIEW:

TOTAL NUMBER CARED FOR IN PROGRAMME:

TARGET GROUP:
(e.g. street children; indicate if children from
specific ethnic groups are targeted)

AGE GROUP:

SEX: ☐ Female   ☐ Male
      ☐ Both

LENGTH OF STAY AT INSTITUTION:

DURATION OF CARE/SUPPORT:
(for those not in institutions)

HOURS OF SERVICE (when do they open and close?):

COMMON HEALTH PROBLEMS/NEEDS OF CHILDREN:
(see physical and psycho-social inventory)

HOW ARE THEY DEALT WITH:

DIFFICULTIES ENCOUNTERED IN DEALING WITH CHILDREN:

DAILY ACTIVITIES:
(describe a typical day at the institution)

WEEKLY/MONTHLY/ANNUAL ACTIVITIES:

WHAT IS REQUIRED OF BENEFICIARIES:

MAIN SOURCES OF FUNDS:

MONITORING AND EVALUATION OF PROGRAMMES:

METHOD OF FOLLOW-UP OF BENEFICIARIES:

COLLABORATING AGENCIES:
- ☐ Governmental
- ☐ University
- ☐ Religious
- ☐ Other, specify
- ☐ Non-governmental
- ☐ Hospital/Clinic
- ☐ Community

SPECIFIC AREAS OF COLLABORATION:

STRENGTHS OF THE ORGANIZATION:

CONSTRAINTS:

FUTURE PLANS:

INFORMATION/DOCUMENTATION AVAILABLE:
(Please list all materials available. Use additional paper if necessary)
Unpublished papers/reports:

Published papers/reports/books:

Bibliographies:

Training materials:

Videos:

Posters:

Others:

ONGOING AND/OR PLANNED RESEARCH:

METHOD OF DISSEMINATING INFORMATION LISTED ABOVE:

WHAT IMPORTANT THINGS SHOULD CHANGE IN YOUR COUNTRY TO PREVENT SEXUAL EXPLOITATION AND SEXUAL ABUSE OF CHILDREN?

WHAT MEASURES IN YOUR OPINION SHOULD BE TAKEN TO HELP SEXUALLY EXPLOITED AND SEXUALLY ABUSED CHILDREN TO CHANGE THEIR SITUATION?

IS THERE ANYTHING ELSE YOU WISH TO ADD?

B. Interview Guide for Health/Social Care Providers

- What is your profession and in which service do you work?

- How long have you worked in this organization? And in this particular service?

- Why do you work in this particular service and how did you begin? What motivates you?

- Are there things you would like to change in your present work?

- What proportion of your patients are sexually exploited or abused children? What proportions of these are male or female?

- What are the most common health problems among the children you see? Among girls? Among boys? (use the health inventory)

- Do you encounter problems associated with or arising from: sexual relations, pregnancy and childbirth, induced abortion, sexually transmitted diseases including HIV infection, AIDS, substance abuse, psychological disorders, developmental delays?

- What difficulties do you face dealing with these children?

- What interventions are included? Play therapy, social skills training etc?

- What procedure do you follow after admitting a child to your centre?

- Do you provide contraceptives or contraceptive information? Do you provide condoms for the prevention of STD/pregnancy? Does your service provide abortion to the children?

- How does a child of either sex have access to your service? Is it through referral or can she/he come directly? Is an appointment necessary? Is the consent of an adult or partner necessary?

- Are some services restricted by age, sex, marital status, ethnic group or citizenship?

- How do you deal with children who cannot be catered for in your programme?

- In a case of referral, where do you refer? How do you follow up the children?

- Do you receive children referred from other centres/organizations?

- To what extent is the service confidential? How many people within the service will have access to the child's name and/or file? Is the individual's name reported for some health matters to others subsequent to the visit?

- Do the children express satisfaction after visiting the service? How is this communicated?

- What are the main barriers to the use of your service by children and what, in your view, could be done to overcome them?

- To what extent do you believe the health problems of sexually abused and exploited children are preventable?

- What, in your opinion, could be done in your service to make it more accessible to sexually abused and exploited children in need?

- What, in your opinion, could be done in your service to make it more effective for sexually abused and exploited children in need?

- Have you had any special training to deal with the special health problems of sexually abused and exploited children? If you have not, would you like to have that opportunity?

HEALTH/SOCIAL CARE FACILITY DIRECT OBSERVATION

Direct observation to assess how health services are actually provided when children are clients. Assess the level and quality of services they receive by using children as clients.

- What (health) services exist, for whom, where, when, why, how much?

- Who brings the children to the (health) centre?

- How accessible is the (health) centre in terms of location?

- Does the centre have a waiting room for children/service users?

- Do the children/service users encounter problems in getting somebody to attend to them?

- For how long do they wait before they are attended to?

- Do they feel at ease with the environment?

- Are there enough posters in and around the premises? What types?

- How explicit are those posters?

- Does the centre have beds, do children have to leave after being attended to or both?

- If they have to leave, how does it deal with serious cases?

- In case of admission, what procedures are followed?

- In a case of referral, where do they refer?

- In which situations do they refer?

- How do they treat cases of referral from other (health) centres?

- What other follow-up do they use after a child/service user leaves the centre?

- Do they have special rooms to deal with children/service users who have personal problems, that is, with more privacy for discussions?

- How many types of services do they offer at the same time?

- Are there specific provisions for dealing with sexually abused and exploited children?

- What are the facilities available at the centre and what are they short of?

- Can the children using the (health) centre come without appointment?

- Do they require anything from the child before they are attended to?

- How do they assist those who cannot, for instance, fill in forms?

- Do they pay for the treatment/service? Do they pay before or after receiving the treatment/service? How much?

- How are children/service users who cannot pay immediately treated/provided care?

- What are the characteristics of the children using the service with regard to age, sex, marital status?

- What difficulties do they face in presenting their problems?

HEALTH FACILITY DIRECT OBSERVATION *(continued)*

- Do they make their requests (personal and medical) known to the (health) workers?

- What are the characteristics of the (health) workers with regard to age, sex and training?

- What is the approach or general attitude of the (health) workers to their duties and the children/service users?

- Are the (health) workers approachable?

- Apart from providing health and social services, do they give advice to patients when necessary, especially sexually abused and exploited children?

- How do the (health) workers decongest the centre of those who are not service users?

- How are the children taken care of in terms of feeding?

- Are there hawkers around who sell food to children/service users who are hungry in the course of receiving treatment/care?

State of physical structures, care and interactions

- Number of buildings and size

- Condition of buildings

- Facilities available: telephone, cooking, bathroom and toilet, sleeping arrangements, clothing, recreation (games, toys and books)

- Approach and attitude of caregivers to their duties and children

– quality of care, hygiene, health and nutrition

– Do children show sign of psychological neglect, inadequate stimulation, malnourishment?

– Does the centre have any contact with community members?

Additional comments:

NAME OF INTERVIEWER/OBSERVER: ....

DATE AND PLACE OF INTERVIEW: ....

C. INTERVIEW GUIDE FOR TEACHERS

- What subjects do you teach? Where do you teach? What grade/age do you teach?

- What are the most common questions children have about sexual abuse and exploitation?

- Do you provide sexual, family life and reproductive health education or information on sexual abuse and exploitation to children?

- If so, of what age and sex?

- Have there been opportunities to involve young people in outlining the education course, and have you made use of young people in any subsequent modifications?

- Have parents been involved in the development or implementation of the activities?

- What are the major lessons you have learned about what makes the education effective?

- Are there opportunities for students to practise skills that would assist them to communicate their feelings and wishes assertively, request assistance, respond to persuasion and deal with threats and violence?

- Do you find it difficult to address issues of sexual abuse and exploitation?

- Do the children find it difficult to discuss these issues?

- What differences in behaviour do you find between the younger and older children?

- What differences in behaviour do you find between the sexes?

- Have you had any special training to deal with sexual abuse and exploitation? If you have not, would you like to have that opportunity?

- Is specific information provided about local health and social services which could meet the needs of sexually abused and exploited children?

- Does the education provide field visits to local health and social services and places where children are engaged in sexual exploitation?

- Is individual counselling provided by you or others in the school which covers sexual abuse and exploitation?

- Have you come across children who are sexually abused or exploited in your school?

- How were they identified and what action was taken?

- Do these children have learning and/or concentration difficulties? Probe for forgetfulness, uneven levels of concentration and difficulties in undertaking simple tasks.

- Do these children socialize with other children in the school easily?

- What other problems do they have that differ from those experienced by other children in your school?

- In your opinion, can the school and teachers play an important role in preventing sexual abuse and exploitation of children? If no, why not? If yes, how?

- What role can the school/teachers play in the reintegration of children who have been sexually abused and/or exploited?

D. INTERVIEW GUIDE FOR CHILDREN – FACTORS AFFECTING HEALTH

- Tell me about yourself. Probe for age, family and educational background, ethnic group, type of work. (See separate paper on page 15 for pointers)
- Describe in detail the setting in which the children live
- Describe in detail the setting in which the children work
- What do you like/dislike about your work?
- Can you leave if you wish to?
- What are your dreams and future aspirations?
- Do you ever think of returning to your family and/or marriage?
- How often do you visit your family?
- What are your daily activities from the moment you wake up to the time you go to sleep? Probe for working/sleeping hours
- Do you have a day off? How do you spend your free time?
- How much money do you earn? How much is kept by the brothel/bar owner and how much do you receive? Do you share the money you earn with others? How much and how often?
- How much of this money do you send to your parents/family?
- At what age did you enter commercial sex? At what age were you sexually abused?
- Were you forced, sold or did you enter "willingly"? If sold or forced, by whom?
- Were any of your family members or close friends and relatives involved? How?
- How long have you been working?
- What type of sexual exploitation are you involved in?
- Do you have someone to turn to for support when in need?
- Do you have friends? How do they define them?
- Do family members, friends and service providers approve of the work you are doing? Why? How is it communicated?
- Have you been physically or sexually abused at your place of work? By whom? How did it happen?
- How many clients do you have per day? Describe them. Probe for age, sex, profession, nationality of the client.
- Do you use condoms during sexual encounters?
- Do you use them all the time or only with some people? If selective, which people and why?
- Have you suffered from STDs previously? or/and been pregnant?
- What did you do? Probe for the decision to abort or deliver the child and how it was made.
- Did you seek care? Where? What was the reaction of your friends, family members and service providers?
- Have you ever taken any substances? Do you take any currently? If yes, which ones?
- Why do you choose these particular substances? Probe for effects, availability and cost.
- What is/are the slang name(s)? How do you take the substance(s)? Probe for methods of using substances.
- How frequently do you use it/them?
- Do different types of children prefer different substances? Probe for substances used by younger/ older children; boys/girls and children in various work contexts.

INTERVIEW GUIDE FOR CHILDREN – CARE UTILIZATION

- What are your medical, psychological and social needs?
- How are your needs/complaints handled by caregivers?
- What preventive methods do you use?
- When do you use health services? Drop-in centres? Rehabilitation centres?
- How frequently do you visit these services?
- When was the last visit? Did you go alone? If no, who accompanied you and why?
- How do you know about these facilities?
- What do you get in terms of services, supplies and advice when do you go there?
- Are there services you do not go to?
- If yes, why? If no, why? Probe for accessibility and acceptability.
- What would you suggest for improving the situation?
- When was the last visit to a doctor?
- What was the diagnosis and length of treatment?
- Was the care and medicine provided free of charge or was there a fee paid?
- If you paid, how much was it and who paid?
- Do you use medicines which were prescribed or suggested by others?
- What kind of help would you wish to have?
- Do you have any recommendations to prevent sexual exploitation and abuse of children in your country?
- What measures should be taken to help victims at various stages of sexual exploitation and sexual abuse?

PROBING THE CHILD'S BACKGROUND AND HISTORY OF ABUSE/EXPLOITATION

History of sexual exploitation/abuse

> description of the child victims in terms of age, sex, socio-economic background, educational level, parents' occupation and educational background, family size, number of siblings, their age and sex, position of victim in family etc

Who the molesters/agents are

> are they adults, strangers, neighbours, someone they know, family members, employers? Probe on how abuse/exploitation took place and the possible reasons. (e.g. a possible cause in domestic sexual abuse is poor marital relationships, death of mother, separation of parents).

Age when molested or when entered commercial sex?

Duration and type of sexual abuse/exploitation

> did it only happen once or was it recurrent? Did the sexual abuse include genital penetration or was it only playing/fondling with genitals? Were the children threatened if they disclosed the abuse/exploitation?

How did they stop/end the sexual abuse/exploitation? What was the reaction of peers, teachers, family members, caregivers, officials etc?

Annex III: Human Resources Development Section, ESCAP

The Economic and Social Commission for Asia and the Pacific is the regional arm of the United Nations for economic and social development in Asia and the Pacific. Established in 1947, it consists of 60 member countries and territories.

Since the adoption by the Commission of the Jakarta Plan of Action on Human Resources Development in the ESCAP Region, the mission of ESCAP in the field of HRD has been to strengthen national capacity to plan and deliver HRD services to the people of Asia and the Pacific. ESCAP defines HRD as a virtuous cycle of investment in human resources to enhance productive capabilities; utilization of those human resources to produce increased and higher-quality output; and consumption by those human resources of the benefits generated by that increased and higher-quality output, thereby leading to an enhanced quality of life. To support countries of Asia and the Pacific in developing their human resources, ESCAP promotes the development of institutions and the enhancement of government performance to promote HRD. Targeted HRD services include education and skills development, employment and health. The ability to read and write, sustain a livelihood, and maintain an adequate standard of health are viewed as basic human entitlements. The main target groups of the programme are government ministries and agencies as well as NGOs working to promote HRD for the poor, women, youth and children in need of special protection measures. The HRD Section of the Social Development Division is the unit primarily responsible for carrying out this mission. In addition, it serves as the United Nations regional focal point for youth-related concerns for Asia and the Pacific, in pursuance of the World Programme of Action for Youth to the Year 2000 and Beyond.

The Section promotes regional cooperation in HRD through intercountry forums, research, training, advisory services and information exchange and networking in the following areas: HRD policy formulation; capacity-building of institutions and national personnel in the public, private and NGO sectors; planning and delivery of HRD services, including basic education and skills development, employment and health; and promotion of "best practices" in HRD.

Intergovernmental services. The Section reports to the annual Commission session and the ESCAP Committee on Socio-economic Measures to Alleviate Poverty in Rural and Urban Areas on the state of HRD in the Asian and Pacific region. In addition, it holds regional meetings on HRD for government and NGO officials, to promote regional cooperation and exchange of experience. The Section also collaborates actively with other United Nations agencies on the implementation of projects, to ensure intersectoral complementarity.

Policy/action research. The Section has established a network of centres of excellence for HRD research and training, comprising over 100 organizations. These institutions, both academic and non-governmental, serve as resources in the region on HRD issues. In addition, the ESCAP HRD Award is presented annually in recognition of exemplary work in the field of HRD. Winners can be either government, NGOs or individuals. Past Award themes have included "Women in poverty", "Employment for youth", "Community development" and "Adult education". The Section also undertakes action-oriented research. In addition to the research on sexual abuse and sexual exploitation summarized in this publication, research has been conducted on various aspects of HRD as well as youth policy formulation and participation.

Curriculum development and training. One of the core areas of the Section's work is the ESCAP HRD Series on Training for Development. This series includes the *ESCAP HRD Course for Poverty Alleviation,* which comprises 11 modules, to address the generic issues of social development, as well as specific poverty alleviation tools and techniques. In addition, the course provides youth leaders and youth work personnel with project management capacity-building to further their work. In 2000, ESCAP will be launching *the ESCAP HRD Course on Medical and Psychosocial Services for Sexually Abused and Sexually Exploited Children and Youth.* This course, which is targeted at health and social service personnel, addresses the medical, psychosocial, HIV/AIDS and substance abuse issues relevant to the effective recovery of sexually abused and sexually exploited young people. Finally, the Section has prepared a Handbook for Literacy and Post-literacy for Women's Empowerment in South Asia as well as a Handbook for Literacy and Post-literacy for Capacity-Building of Organizations, in cooperation with UNESCO. These Handbooks provide support to literacy personnel to enable them to manage their literacy and post-literacy programmes more effectively.

Public information. The HRD Section produces a biannual newsletter, targeted mainly at government officials, NGOs and academic institutions. The newsletter features interviews with opinion leaders, updates about the Section's work and HRD country profiles. In order to provide information to the general public, the Section's maintains its own web site *(<www.escap-hrd.org>).* The web site contains information on the work of the HRD Section, articles pertaining to health, education and employment, HRD resources, fact sheets on Asia and the Pacific, newsletter articles, and publications.

Annex IV: Section for International Maternal and Child Health, Uppsala University, Sweden

The Section for International Maternal and Child Health, which is collaborating with ESCAP in the project, falls under the Department of Women's and Children's Health at the Faculty of Medicine of Uppsala University, Sweden.

The Section was established in 1977 with the objective of carrying out research and training programmes that are relevant to the promotion of child health and development, with a special emphasis on low-income countries. With its multidisciplinary staff, the Section brings together a broad perspective on the child, ranging from paediatric care and child health to maternal health, nutrition, nursing, rehabilitation and social sciences, as well as health education, health-care management and information. This creates a critical mass of expertise that is suitable for the establishment of partnerships with research and training institutions in low-income countries. The Section's fields of activities are training, research, advisory services and consultancies, library and documentation and information services.

Training. The Section arranges regular courses for students from Sweden and abroad. An extensive training programme is offered, comprising individual courses and a master's programme to more than 300 students annually. An example of an individual course that is offered annually by the Section is "Medical and psychosocial services for children in especially difficult circumstances in low-income countries". The aim of the course is to provide social and health-care providers with knowledge of the medical and psycho-social needs and problems of children in general and children in especially difficult circumstances in particular, and to promote skills in the design, management and evaluation of services that adequately address them. The course also addresses the challenge of combining preventive and remedial measures in a manner that stimulates team-work between medical, psychological and social caregivers. The course adopts an active learning approach whereby participants are assisted in conducting their own analysis of a priority care problem in their own institutions, developing a project to address the problem, deciding on a monitoring and evaluation guide, and then implementing their own solution to the problem identified over an eight-month period.

Research. The Section has a long-standing tradition of research related to health care in low-income countries dating from the 1960s. Today, the research activities can be grouped under the following areas: child health services, social paediatrics and international nutrition.

Advisory services and consultancies. The Section has carried out a range of consultancy and advisory activities for agencies such as Sida, ESCAP, UNICEF, FAO and WHO, as well as NGOs. The activities reflect the skills and interests of the academic staff and comprise participation in the planning, implementation and evaluation of health programmes at various levels of health care. The staff frequently give technical advice to those working with child health issues in low-income countries. The Section is currently a partner in a number of bilateral programmes comprising research and training. One such programme is the Sida-supported project on strengthening national HRD capabilities through training of social service and health personnel to combat sexual abuse and sexual exploitation of children and youth in the Greater Mekong Subregion, which is being implemented by ESCAP in collaboration with the Section. It also collaborates with institutions in the United Republic of Tanzania and Zimbabwe.

Library and documentation. The Section's library has a unique collection of books and periodicals covering the field of health care in low-income countries. It comprises some 4,500 titles and 150 periodicals on primary health care, child health, nutrition, obstetrics and gynaecology, family planning, nutrition, rehabilitation and health education. The library is registered in LIBRIS (the union of catalogue of Swedish libraries) and can thus be easily accessed from all over Scandinavia. Much of the material is not available elsewhere in Sweden. The library also has bibliographic databases on children in exceptionally difficult circumstances and disability in low-income countries.

Information Services. The information activities of the Section are mainly focused on the review journal NU – News on Health Care in Developing Countries. NU is published four times a year and issued to some 130 countries. Its thematic approach spans the whole area of health care in low-income countries, such as safe motherhood, rehabilitation, HIV/AIDS and commercial sexual exploitation of children. A directory of training courses, covering some 200 courses around the world is published annually. Information to the media is also part of the information services.

References

Cambodia Red Cross and Australian Red Cross, 1997. *Sexual Knowledge, Attitudes and Behaviour in Cambodia and the Threat of Sexually Transmitted Diseases* (Phnom Penh).

Global Alliance Against Trafficking in Women, International Organisation for Migration and Cambodian Women's Development Association, 1997. *Two Reports on the Situation of Women and Children Trafficked from Cambodia and Viet Nam to Thailand* (Bangkok).

Seaman, T., 1995. *Research Report on Child Prostitution and Trafficking in Battambang,* Cambodian League for the Promotion and Defence of Human Rights (Phnom Penh).

United Nations Children's Fund, 1995. *The Trafficking and Prostitution of Children in Cambodia: A Situation Report* (Phnom Penh).

————, 1998. *Towards a Better Future: An analysis of the Situation of Children and Women in Cambodia* (Phnom Penh).

United Nations Development Programme, 1998. *Human Development Report 1998* (New York Oxford University Press).